IMMANUEL

When God Was One of Us

Thoughts on Advent

April Bumgardner

Every Leaf Press™

© 2020 April Bumgardner

First edition

Every Leaf Press™

All rights reserved. No part of this book may be reproduced in any form without permission in writing, except in the case of brief quotations attributed to the author.

All Scripture quotations are taken from the Holy Bible, English Standard Version® (ESV®), copyright © 2001 by Crossway, a publishing ministry of Good News Publishers. Used by permission. All rights reserved.

Cover design: Lee Ann Lamb

Name: Bumgardner, April, author.

Title: Immanuel: When God Was One of Us, Thoughts on Advent / April Bumgardner.

Description: First edition | Every Leaf Press,™ [2020] |

      Includes biographical notes.

Identifiers: ISBN 978-0-578-72806-3

Subjects: Advent - Christmas - devotional - incarnation - image of God - preparation - Holy Spirit

Any grammatical or theological error is the responsibility of the author. Any truth or beauty found within these pages belongs solely to the glory of God.

For more information regarding the author and Every Leaf Press,™ go to

www.lovingeveryleaf.com

Printed in the United States of America

For Stephen M. Kenney,
because of his Stream sermon series

And for William,
who first brought me coffee over twenty-five years ago

Contents

Preface | 1

Introduction | 3

December 1   Preparation | 6

December 2   Plot Points | 9

December 3   Someone Is Coming | 13

December 4   The Innumerable Stars and the Westward Star | 17

December 5   Like Me | 23

December 6   Justice and Mercy | 27

December 7   A Message for All Nations | 32

December 8   Good News | 38

December 9   Word of Wonder | 44

December 10   Light | 48

December 11	Once Before Time	52
December 12	Let It Be	56
December 13	They Made Known the Saying	63
December 14	Remembering	67
December 15	The Incarnation in Suffering	73
December 16	The Holy Immigrant	80
December 17	Dignity	88
December 18	God Is One of Us	94
December 19	Ridiculous	99
December 20	New	103
December 21	No Excuses	110
December 22	The Body of Christ	115
December 23	Living Generously	119
December 24	Holy Spirit	125

December 25   Christmas Day | 130

December 26   Final Advent | 134

Biographical Notes | 138

Preface

Christmas is a favorite time of year for many people, and for many, it is the most stressful and depressing. My desire is that this book may be an encouragement to both. In acknowledging both the joy and the anguish of the season, we honor our dependence and need for God in a genuine way. It is my hope that this daily devotional will help quiet and focus our minds and hearts to celebrate and worship the Savior who came down to be one of us.

Many Advent books follow traditional and thematic readings, such as hope, joy, peace, and love. This one does not. I have chosen, instead, to organize the topics roughly in the following way: the problem of sin and death, the prophets and preparation, the chronology of the events of Jesus' birth, and the implications and applications of the incarnation.

I have also decided not to follow a traditional Advent calendar. Many of them cover the four weeks before Christmas and provide readings for the twelve days of Christmas. To simplify and allow for readings multiple years, I begin these devotionals on the first day of December. There is one reading for each day through Christmas, plus a last reading on December 26. This final reading is to remind us that, while our anticipation for his first coming is complete, we still live in joyful hope for his second and final coming.

How you choose to read these daily devotionals is entirely up to you. It may depend on your season of life, or the faith tradition you are most comfortable with. You may read them quietly to yourself in the morning, light candles with your family in the evenings, discuss them in community, include extra readings, or listen to music as accompaniment. The choice is yours. In whatever way you participate, I pray you experience the truth of his presence, and eagerly await with me his final Advent.

Introduction

On the other hand, we admit that history… is a story written by the finger of God.
    -C. S. Lewis in Christian Reflections

We are all chosen, broken creatures and Jesus has made us all into artists, whether we use a brush or simply ride on a garbage truck. Our stories are living stories of the Kingdom that we write every day. Infused with the mystery of the Great Artist's spirit, our stories can become a wide open adventure—part of the Greatest Story Ever Told.

    -Makoto Fujimura in his blog post "Manger, Magi and the Mystery of Majesty" at https://www.makotofujimura.com/writings/manger-magi-and-the-mystery-of-majesty/

The most beautiful story ever written was not written down initially, but rather created, imagined and fleshed out from the eternal mind of God. This perfect narrative, lovely and full of love, was created plot point by plot point, from one tragic garden scene to another, from wandering rejected forefathers and prophets, to a rejected one who is more than a prophet, the uncreated Son of the Father. The most beautiful story ever written was the culmination of God's created narrative in the man Jesus. But the story does not begin with Jesus as a man, but rather comes to its narrative climax after thousands of years of promises and foreshadowing.

The story does not suddenly change; there is no surprising twist, but the crescendo of God's incarnation was long planned and long expected. We just missed the signs. Are we still missing the signs?

Do we read Genesis, Deuteronomy and Amos, then sigh with relief when we get to the tenderness of Jesus? He never changed the plot. He didn't lighten or deviate from the narrative. The tenderness was always there. God always had this very story in mind. It is the most beautiful story ever written because it was well conceived, from beginning to end, from the incomparable heart of God. God, the Author and Creator, came down to be one of us.

In this little devotional book, I pray I effectively interact with the text of Scripture. However, in a secondary way, I want to interact with the thoughts of others as they have responded over time and joined in the conversation regarding Scripture and its glorious climax: the life and personhood of Jesus Christ. This is one reason I have included quotes as headings for each of the daily readings. Another reason is that I love to introduce dear friends to one another. If you are already acquainted, then I am even more pleased, yet feel it is worthwhile to remind you of their wonderful existence. Though I have not met these friends personally (and perhaps I've not met you either, friend!), I have found something valuable in their words. And like friends I do know, I do not necessarily agree with these authors in everything. Only Scripture is infallible, but I believe there are many beautiful truths represented here. Most of the people, but not all, included in these curated quotes are followers of Jesus and have spent much of their lives struggling to discover and plumb the depths of what it means for the divine to become human, and for humanity to stretch toward the divine.

Likewise, I pray that not only do I interact with the text of Scripture, but also with the great Word himself. In some respects, it can become easy to elevate the canon of the Bible over and above God himself to the point that we worship the physical book. This may seem a fine distinction, but I think it is an appropriate one to make. The Bible is a narrative acquired through people, but ultimately from God. We worship God alone and follow him in Spirit and in truth. His Spirit guides the formation of history, the writings and translations of his word, full of truth, goodness and beauty. Yet, his Spirit still remains hovering over us and in us as we read. Thus, my prayer is that in this little devotional book for Advent, I faithfully interact with the Holy Spirit and his community.

Let's hear his story and marvel at its perfect beauty. Then, let us tap a shoulder, guide a wounded heart to a mug of tea or hot coffee and retell it imperfectly, inevitably messing up bits here and there, but keeping the love, the truth, the goodness and the beauty intact.

December 1

Preparation

Advent is not the kind of preparation that involves shopping and parties and cards. Such illusions of abundance disguise the true cravings of our weary souls.
   -Walter Brueggeman in Celebrating Abundance

While the term Advent means "the coming," its significance for us takes on a few different meanings. First, we recognize as believers that the Messiah has already come. At one historical point, he has already been born, lived his life, died and been exalted for us. We no longer await a Savior, for he has come. Yet, in another sense, we do wait. We believe that the very same Messiah is coming. Jesus the Christ, whom the prophets foretold and in whom the angels rejoiced, is coming again as he promised. One day, not yet determined by human time, the Son of God will return and usher in the culmination of God's plan: bringing a people home to a forever-redeemed relationship with him. In this sense, he is coming, and in this sense, we also wait for him. However, this is not the Advent of Christmas.

A Christmas Advent is a metaphorical coming. We practice and prepare for this ultimate coming by remembering the first. Some of us sing carols of a humble birth, light candles or read the second chapter of the Gospel of Luke in order to prepare our minds and hearts for remembering his coming as an infant into a Jewish home, in a tumultuous political climate, in a small pocket of the ancient world.

Advent is a coming. It is a waiting, and while we wait, we prepare. When our family prepares for someone to visit, we tidy the house, we steam mop the floors, and we cook a meal. This helps our guests know they are expected and welcomed. However, the type of preparation Advent calls for is different. It is a quieting of the mind, an opening of the heart. Some may choose to clear their calendars of the typical and distracting busyness of the holiday season. Others may set aside family time for reflective reading and discussion. Regardless of how you choose to honor his coming, Advent requires preparation.

At this time of year, during the season of Advent, let us honor those who came long before us by imitating the hope they held in their hearts for God to send his own to us. Let us, likewise, recognize that the baby no longer lies in the feeding trough, but reigns supreme on his own eternal throne. Exalted forever, Jesus will leave that throne only once more to gather us all, not in a metaphorical sense, but in a literal collection. He will welcome all peoples before their Creator.

Even youths shall faint and be weary,

and young men shall fall exhausted;

but they who wait for the LORD shall renew their strength;

they shall mount up with wings like eagles;

they shall run and not be weary;

they shall walk and not faint.

(Isaiah 40:30-31)

***

Dear Lord,

Quiet our hearts this season. Help us to fight against the busyness of the culture and wait for you. Teach us the lessons that are learned with waiting.

In Jesus' name,

Amen.

Reflections:

1. How will I choose to prepare for this Advent? What would be most meaningful for me? What could I choose to help quiet my heart, not just to fill my calendar?
2. What provides me the greatest hope?

December 2

Plot Points

According to most philosophers, God in making the world enslaved it. According to Christianity, in making it, He set it free. God had written, not so much a poem, but rather a play; a play he had planned as perfect, but which had necessarily been left to human actors and stage-managers, who had since made a great mess of it.

-G. K. Chesterton in Orthodoxy

In the beginning there was simply God. He was three personalities in one. His Spirit hovered mysteriously over the water. It is unclear where the water came from, or even the void, but the opening verses of Genesis, and indeed the whole inspired Bible, fills us with the expectancy of something new. Initially, it was all good. The trees, the birds, the clouds, the system of a flowing sense of time; it was all good. For a brief moment, God critiques his own work when man is alone. Even in his critique, however, he has an immediate remedy: woman. And it is all good again, full of potential and promise and intimacy. God's gift of life is accompanied by freedom and possibility.

Humanity is given a garden, a task within a beautiful place to live and walk with God. Adam's and Eve's days are filled with tending to the flourishing of their world. Their evenings are spent in unimaginable communion with the Creator as they walk together in the "cool of the evening."

When evil enters paradise, however, disobedience slips in, and fear, and shame and guilt. The intimacy is broken, and God must protect us from ourselves. Again, he is not without a remedy. But this remedy would be more involved. Its implementation would require multiple plot points in the narrative God had initially planned for his creation.

Although human history seems to cycle viciously, independently and recklessly on its own accord, God still maintains his sovereignty. From the serpent's first hiss and the woman's first lie and taste and swallow, God has himself authored the narrative. While he grants us the privilege of free will and creative liberty, he has given us the structure and scaffolding around which to return to his story, the one closest to the intended original. He does not abandon creation in its belligerence but upholds it. He propped it up in its wounded, broken state until we can be healed and made right with him once more. This is God's story for us. This is the narrative story and promise of the Bible.

Plot point by plot point, we see the finger of God move through the text. He creates, edits and, in his vulnerability, rewrites the grand epic so we can still be his loving focus.

Plot point 1 - God creates and pours all his creativity and love into formation of the earth, the waters and the heavens. His very breath enlivens us.

Plot point 2 - Humanity's rejection of God results in brokenness. Humanity creates a chasm that cannot easily be crossed. With each passing day, each subsequent generation, we only widen the chasm. The Creator and Author alone can span it.

Plot point 3 - God gives the covenant. God quickly promises his ability and desire to protect us and bring us back. We are still broken and expelled from our close communion, but he whispers of someone to come.

Plot point 4 - God works with the people and the prophets. Through his sovereignty and love, the Creator forms a protected people and sends his messengers over hundreds of years to remind us of the help that is assuredly coming.

Plot point 5 - The Christ is here! All is restored and rectified and made right. Almost.

Plot point 6 - He is coming again. So we wait, not in idleness, but in expectancy, full of preparation, imitating him as we hover in our own weak ways of creativity. In this Advent, we rejoice as we prepare for his promised and inevitable coming.

Concerning this salvation, the prophets who prophesied about the grace that was to be yours searched and inquired carefully.... He was foreknown before the foundation of the world but was made manifest in the last times for the sake of you who through him are believers in God. (I Peter 1:10, 20 - 21)

Who is this that would come? How would he accomplish this healing reunion? How long do we have to wait?
***

Oh, dear Creator, forgive us for turning our back on you. Forgive us for stubbornly rejecting your original narrative. We long for communion with you once more. Please help us to wait patiently for the arrival of the remedy you have long planned for us.

Reflections:

1. How would I articulate the Biblical story in a few sentences?
2. What sort of image of God does this reading conjure for me? Is it different from how I usually think of God?

December 3

Someone Is Coming

I take literally the statement in the Gospel of John that God loves the world. I believe that the world was created and approved by love, that it subsists, coheres, and endures by love, and that, insofar as it is redeemable, it can be redeemed only by love. I believe that divine love, incarnate and indwelling in the world, summons the world always toward wholeness, which ultimately is reconciliation and atonement with God.

-Wendell Berry in Another Turn of the Crank

When Adam and Eve chose their own ignorance over God's eternal wisdom and divine love, the Creator expelled them from the beautiful garden in which he talked with them tenderly and regularly. He did not expel them out of anger or vengeance, but from a deep desire to bring them back. His primary motivation is love. He always acts out of love. The Creator refused to live with them in a hurtful, false and broken relationship, so he chose to redeem them. In redeeming Adam and Eve, he knew he would be redeeming their children and all future generations. God, in his great love, allowed himself to be vulnerable. Vulnerability is by no means a sign of God's weakness, but instead, his willingness to be bruised and betrayed because of his love. He chose vulnerability so that humanity would have the freedom to choose him. Yet when they chose themselves, God did not abandon them. Rather, in banishing Adam and Eve from the garden and easy perfect communion with him, God took the first step in bringing us all back home to him and bringing us back into healthy relationships with one another.

There were dire consequences. God disclosed the pain and anguish and oppression humanity was to suffer due to their rejection of the Creator. And then, there, amid punitive-sounding utterances God pronounced the first promise, the beginning of hope. Here we lay aside the discussion of whether or not this serpent was Satan, or a mere representation of evil, whether or not Adam and Eve were true literal humans, or whether they represented early humanity. Instead, we focus on the love of God for his creation and his immediate response to it. Addressing the lying serpent, God spoke to all of humanity. "I'm sending someone to help. I am coming."

I will put enmity between you and the woman, and between your offspring and her offspring; he shall bruise your head, and you shall bruise his heel. (Genesis 3:15)

In our starkest pain and our lowest points, God is there with us, not condemning us, but rescuing us in our self-inflicted condemnation. Christ's promised coming is, indeed, good news. It is the gospel, a proclamation of the ultimate Savior and helper. However, it is only good news if we fully comprehend the profundity of our brokenness. Adam and Eve did not just eat a piece of fruit; they rejected their relationship with the Creator. They preferred their own false sense of sovereignty to the One that could provide true life.

Unfortunately, we are no different. While we differentiate between murder and screaming at someone in traffic, they both separate us from our beautiful communion with God. We have learned from those who have preceded us, and we have taught ourselves to drift further and further away. We choose our way and our desires and, in turn, alienate ourselves further from the goodness of God. Even when this is not our intention, our stubbornness for a kind of knowledge and control stands in the way of our close, experiential knowledge of God. We don't simply long to know about God, but to know deeply, intimately who he is.

The bad news must be first plainly understood: the nurturing and trusting relationship we crave as humans is impossible. We have wrecked it. The good news is this: with God, it is possible. He has promised. He is sending someone. He is coming.

As God continues to record his narrative through the Semitic people, and then in the New Testament through others throughout the Mediterranean world, there is a mystery unfolding. How does

God interact with all peoples? Who is he sending to bruise the serpent's head? Who is coming to help us become friends with God once more? Awaiting the promised one's arrival is only good news if we have already understood our desperate need.

***

Dear God,

We acknowledge we have broken the relationship with you. We don't know how to find our way back to community with you. Forgive us for our stubbornness, arrogance, resentment and faithlessness. Help us to look eagerly for the help you are sending. Help us to be thankful that you have sent the promised one.
Amen.

Reflections:

1. In what ways am I holding on to my own false sovereignty? Is there something I need to relinquish?
2. How does my attitude change knowing God is with me?

December 4

The Innumerable Stars and the Westward Star

I am the sort of Christian whose patriotism might be called into question by some on the grounds that I do not take the United States to be more beloved of God than France, let us say, or Russia, or Argentina, or Iran. I experience religious dread whenever I find myself thinking that I know the limits of God's grace, since I am utterly certain it exceeds any imagination a human being might have to it. God does, after all, so love the world.

-Marilynne Robinson in When I Was a Child I Read Books

O, Star of wonder, star of night,
Star with royal beauty bright,
Westward leading, still proceeding,
Guide us to thy perfect Light.

-John Henry Hopkins, Jr. from the carol "We Three Kings"

"May the Lord be the first one in the car," she prayed, "and the last out."

- Isabel Wilkerson in The Warmth of Other Suns

Out of wealth and comfort, away from family ties and security, and far from the familiar predictable culture of home, God called them. And he used the stars. The innumerable stars of a quiet desert night, and one star peculiarly pulsing ahead. God was determined that his redemptive narrative was to include people, a smattering of the people he was calling back to himself.

He spoke and showed the innumerable stars to Abram, a man of the illustrious ancient city of Ur. The irony of Abram's situation did not escape the Lord. The Lord loves irony. Abram, who was surrounded by family members of significant social standing, was called out of everything he knew, to trust in the Lord who would reveal himself to the man in some undisclosed location. On the journey, Abram and Sarai realize they are unable to have children. Away from family, away from comfortable understanding of how society is structured, Abram and his wife wander, waiting to see how this new Lord would fulfill the seemingly impossible.

"O Lord God, what will you give me, for I continue childless…?"

[The Lord] brought [Abram] outside and said, "Look toward heaven, and number the stars, if you are able to number them…. So shall your offspring be." (Genesis 15:2, 5)

Uncountable stars? Innumerable offspring? What sort of God made such promises? Abram, or Abraham, would soon see it was a God of love, of promises fulfilled, of defying possibilities.

[The Lord] also said to him, "I am the Lord who brought you out of Ur of the Chaldeans to give you this land to take possession of it." (Genesis 15:7)

He was a God who did not take stock in the origins of people, but only in where they were going, only in the part they would play in helping him bring about his original garden promise, how they would help reconstruct his intended narrative.

Then Abram recalled the Lord's first words to him when he beckoned him from all the world he had known:

"Go from your country and your kindred and your father's house....
I will make of you a great nation, and I will bless you and make your name great, so that you will be a blessing.... and in you all the families of the earth shall be blessed." (Genesis 12:1-3)

God was preparing a man to father a nation, but as Abram gazed at the night sky did he question what the stars had to do with any of it?

A couple thousand years pass before another caravan, composed of foreigners divinely called from their home, gaze wonderingly and expectantly at the stars. This time, however, instead of a journey under the innumerable stars of the night sky, they travel, hopefully, keeping their eyes on the scrolls they carry, and their eyes on one, mysterious Westward star. A slow, night-time journey westward takes them also away from loved ones, unsure of the accuracy of their astronomical prophecies and readings. They cannot know exactly what is to come. Little expecting they were part of any grander plan than what they had already conjured for themselves, the Magi (were they ancient astrologers, or eastern kings?) became an integral part of the narrative of the Jewish Messiah. They, too, heard the voice of God, albeit in a dream.

The Gospel of Matthew emphasizes the Jewishness of Jesus. He opens the narrative with a genealogy that demonstrates his undeniable Jewishness going all the way back to Abraham. Yet, the Jewish nation was created by God from a man pulled out of a foreign people, from the Chaldeans (pre-Babylonians, in fact). The Magi were invited by God through a special star they followed in the East to witness a birth. Instead of scoffing at a lowly birth and an unfortunate people, they mounted camels, packed costly gifts, and journeyed west to Jerusalem, then south to the insignificant village of Bethlehem.

When God plans out his story, he plans for all people to be involved. He plans out the roles in unexpected ways. God calls the outlier and protects his travels. God takes the foreigner and makes him the father and fellow citizen of many. God calls the wanderer and sends him out on a circuitous journey. From early on, God's plan was for the world, and though he set aside one man and created a nation, it was the entire world that was blessed.

There were innumerable stars on that quiet, desert night, and they all pointed to the one promised in the garden. There was one mysterious star leading them westward, and their journey fills us all with hope.

***

Dear Father,

We trust in your plan. Though the way seems tumultuous and unsure, we know it is your story you are telling, and you are in control of each part of the tale. Thank you for calling us out of what we have always known. Thank you for showing us we can trust in your hand to guide us even if the journey seems circuitous and foreign, or uncomfortable. Father, be with us as we hope in that star which once shone so brightly. Thank you that you have been with us the entire way.

In Christ's name,

Amen.

Reflections:

1. What are the things in my life that I don't understand right now? Can I trust God to guide me?
2. How can I be more inclusive with the Gospel this Advent? What does that look like?

December 5

Like Me

The nativity mystery, "conceived from the Holy Spirit and born from the Virgin Mary," means that God became human.... Jesus Christ is not only truly God, he is human like every one of us. He is human without limitation. He is not only similar to us, he is like us.

    -Karl Barth in Dogmatics in Outline

When God calls together a people, they are his people, indeed. Although they be disjointed, disgruntled, unfortunate and marginalized, they belong to him. They may not know their own relevance or worth; even so, they are set aside for great purposes. In fact, throughout Scripture the ones whom God has called have often been the unlikeliest of characters—the second born, a shepherd, a weeping prophet, the ostracized son of a profligate, a foreigner, a foul-mouthed fisherman, a discarded and sharp-tongued woman.

Once upon a time God called a Hebrew hiding in the desert, guiding sheep among a foreign people. He called Moses out of his renegade status to rescue a people who only held the promise of nationhood. The Jews were still slaves back in Egypt, forgotten tribes, abandoned by pharaohs and those with empirical power. Moses was a good shepherd, a guide, a judge, a savior, a redeemer. He was adopted into the pharaoh's, own family, part of the royal court, only to reject it for something lowlier.

God called Moses out of his hiding place to be his servant. When Moses complained of his lack of speaking abilities and leadership skills, God ignored his excuses. "You will be my voice," commanded the Lord. "I will give you words to say."

Fifteen-hundred years later God sent the promised Word. He was a good shepherd, a perfect guide, a mediator, a savior, and a redeemer. He left the heavenly courts and his throne above, was adopted into the family of a carpenter, and walked dusty trails. He was the Word who spoke freely and full of grace and truth.

Before the Word appeared, however, Moses gathered the people together. They were now Israelites, the people of God, because they had been called out of Egypt. They were his children in the desert, and Moses spoke with them, promising a future helper who would speak the words of Truth.

"The Lord your God will raise up for you a prophet like me from among you, from your brothers—it is to him you shall listen." (Deuteronomy 18:15)

God was too far away, too removed from empires, and slavery, from frailty and sinfulness and death. The people no longer walked with their God comfortably in the cool of the evening. They had no memory of the garden, nor their relationship with him. They were afraid in their ignorance and stubbornness and brokenness. They craved someone they could approach. They needed someone like Moses, even after their fallible leader succumbed to death. God agreed.

"I will raise up for them a prophet like you from among their brothers. And I will put my words in his mouth, and he shall speak to them all that I command him." (Deuteronomy 18:18)

And so Joshua became the Lord's spokesperson whom the Israelites could approach without fear. Elijah came, then Isaiah and Hosea and Amos and Zechariah. They were not enough. They were insufficient. God had more words to say. Then, when all the needful words were spoken, God, out of his longing and love for us, wanted to come himself. But the people were terrified, so instead, he came like Moses. Like me, like you. He came laughing at his own jokes, reaching out to touch the hurting, and befriending the lonely. According to the

Father's great purposes, this prophet like me, called the marginalized out from the fringes and brought them to God, whole and reunited.

No one has ever seen God, but the one and only Son who is himself God and is in closest relationship with the Father, has made him known. (John 1:18)

***

Dear Father,

Thank you for calling us and forming us. We thank you for being a God of compassion and patience. Thank you for not only intervening in human history, but also becoming a part of it. Thank you for coming close and becoming like us. Help us to draw close to you and to one another.

Reflections:

1. Do I find comfort in the fact that God's Son became like us? Why is that so important to me?
2. How can I draw closer to God this Advent?

December 6

Justice and Mercy

For children are innocent and love justice, while most of us are wicked and naturally prefer mercy.

    -G. K. Chesterton in Orthodoxy

While empires were built and destroyed, and civilizations progressed and made great advances, humanity deteriorated spiritually because they had distanced themselves far away from a time of communion and peace. They no longer shared a memory of a common Creator. God had not forgotten us. However, he spoke to people on occasion reminding them of his good promise and confirming his character. The Lord is just and merciful, holy and full of love. We would not listen.

    Among all the prophets, the words of Amos read the closest to our contemporary situation in the West, particularly in the United States. Wealthy, myopic, and politically stable, the Israelites lived their lives smugly in a check-list fashion, never imagining God might be demanding more from them than cursory actions in the temple. In their xenophobia and pettiness, they would not realize God ached to move closer to them. The Israelites ignored all the repercussions of a faithful relationship with God, not believing God longed for an intimacy with them. He wanted to see that reflected in their interactions with one another. They assumed their strength was proof of their moral fiber, and that geography and name protected them from poverty, or invasion, or even accountability.

Amos was a shepherd and a caretaker of sycamore-fig trees. He was tied to the land. His status as the Lord's prophet reminds us that God uses men of court in tumultuous times, priests who must wander, and men of lowly vocation in times of well-being. The Lord's Messiah will one day be raised as a carpenter in an occupied territory, but will eventually be named a prince, a king, a priest, but also a good shepherd.

Aram, Philistia, Phoenicia, Edom, Ammon and Moab are all systematically chastised for their evil ways. God speaks through Amos to denounce cruelty and idolatry. Amos proclaims God's great expectations for peoples of all nations to live as he created them to be: just and righteous. God punishes all nations, because they all belong to him. As Amos continues, Israel is able to sit comfortably while their enemies are condemned. Then, Judah is named. It is hard to ignore the accusations against their brothers, but still, Amos does not stop.

God reminds them that he has sent many like them to draw them back to God, but they have not listened.

In a land full of food and wealth and plenty, they have chosen to ignore the poor, belittle the oppressed and fear the defenseless. Although God reminds them of who he is and what he wants, they choose not to listen. They busy themselves with the marketplaces, and defend their own rights in the courts, and God rejects their religious gestures.

> I hate, I despise your feasts,
> and I take no delight in your
> solemn assemblies.
> Even though you bring me your
> burnt offerings and grain offerings,
> I will not accept them.
> (Amos 5:21-22a)

The Lord is holy, and he created the world to be holy for him. But we treat it and one another vilely. Amos reminds Israel—and us—to be holy, because that is who God is. He instructs us to be just—full of rightness—because we reflect the Lord's image in our creatureliness. He tells us how to do this: do not seek comfort or the success of the marketplace. Stop seeking monetary gain, or physical accumulations. Seek the Lord to live. Let's walk away from the buying and selling frenzy. Let's reject the tight-fisted anxiety of what is "mine." Let's trade in our fear of want and scarcity, and instead, recognize the image of God also present in the other before us.

> Take away from me the noise of your songs;
> to the melody of your harps I will not listen.
> But let justice roll down like waters,
> and righteousness like an ever-flowing stream.
> (Amos 5:23-24)

While we wait for the Lord's promise, how are we to be? We are to be full of justice and righteousness, two sides of the same coin. We are to be open and compassionate and effusive in our giving. We are to be like God to the others before us.

While we wait, Amos reminds us to honor God's image, and in the ever-flowing waters of righteousness, to reflect that back to others.

While we wait, we are not idle.

***

Holy Father,

You are the ever-flowing stream of righteousness and justice. You see the poor and abused and act rightly. We ask your forgiveness when we refuse to see both the human and the divine in our neighbors.

Reflections:

1. Who are the oppressed and defenseless in my world? How could I extend justice and mercy to them?
2. How has God shown me forgiveness?

December 7

A Message for All Nations

If we did not believe that truth is universal, why should so many missionaries endure these hardships? It is precisely because truth is common to all countries and all times that we call it truth. If a true doctrine were not true alike in Portugal and Japan we could not call it true.
    -Shusaku Endo

Stille Nacht, heilige Nacht   *Silent night, holy night*
Alles schläft; einsam wacht.   *All is calm, all is bright.*
    -Josef Mohr (translated by John Freeman Young)

If God wishes to speak clearly, he will speak clearly. If he wishes to use the vocabulary of humanity in multiple ways, on the other hand, he will. His prophets (Amos, Hosea, Ezekiel, Malachi, Zechariah) often saw confusing visions from the Lord—of plumb lines and fiery wheels, of dry bones and baskets of fruits—and they struggled to make sense of it in the Lord's presence. They understood they were God's messengers for that time, in that place, and recognized they were speaking his revelation and truth to Judah in their arrogance, Israel in captivity or Nineveh in their wickedness. How could they have predicted John the Baptist, his beard sticky with honey, or a sketchy fisherman preaching of a risen Savior while a tongue of fire danced above his head? These men were not given to know how far their words would stretch. How could they know their message and influence would extend across an ocean to a continent still unknown to them, or over on to islands far east of them?

God sent his messengers to speak a word to his wayward people but layered it with meanings that could be peeled back over time to eventually reveal their ultimate fulfillment in the Messiah. Isaiah spoke of his own wife giving birth as a gift, but it was not until that day centuries later, after Caesar Augustus had issued a decree, that God became one of us in Bethlehem, and finally fulfilled the prophecy in its entirety (Isaiah 7:14). God always speaks the truth, but he himself is the Truth.

Approximately five-hundred years before the Christ-child was born, a priestly prophet was called in Judah to encourage the people to rebuild the temple after returning from captivity, and to remind them to watch for a certain Messiah. This coming Messiah would be holy but human, a man yet sent from God. Astoundingly, he would be a "priest on his throne" (Zechariah 6:13). However peculiar this sounded to the ancient Jews—a priestly king—it would certainly be that much more unusual for us today in the West in the twenty-first century. Although our nations have attempted to keep religion and state-sovereignty separate from one another, we have adulterated them into a preposterous mix which taints one and misrepresents the other.

Yet Zechariah assures Judah that "the counsel of peace shall be between them both" (Zechariah 6:13). In the habitual injustice of human societies and the power struggle of politics, where would God find a place? Zechariah tells us that there will be a Kingdom where God is sovereign, and he will not share his throne with oppressors. There will not be an imbalance of power, because the Lord alone will rule triumphantly with justice, mercy and compassion (Zechariah 7:9). Instead, this young prophet declares something shocking beyond words: the Lord promises to live among them!

"Shout and be glad, Daughter Zion. For I am coming, and I will live among you," declares the Lord. "Many nations will be joined with the Lord in that day and will become my people. I will live among you and you will know that the Lord Almighty has sent me to you." (Zechariah 2:10-11)

How does God live among us? He stripped himself of glory, put on muscle and tendon, and walked among a discarded nation and a conflicted society. Judah hears that they are not forgotten. There is yet hope and mercy from the Lord. May we hear the same beautiful message! If she is careful, Judah will not miss another great promise, a promise of international community. Let us make sure twenty-five hundred years later we do not miss it either. In case we did not hear, another visionary reminds us several hundred years after Zechariah, while describing God's temple and city and kingdom.

> I did not see a temple in the city, because the Lord God Almighty and the Lamb are its temple. The city does not need the sun or the moon to shine on it, for the glory of God gives it light, and the Lamb is its lamp. The nations will walk by its light, and the kings of the earth will bring their splendor into it. (Revelation 21:22-24)

Zechariah and John both promise in their revelations that though we appreciate our individual heritages and cultures, we speak varied languages, and adhere to sundry political systems, ultimately, we will be gathered again to the throne of God and his kingdom. We will not be divided by nationhood but live harmoniously together with our awaited King who will pitch his tent among us eternally.

> And I heard a loud voice from the throne saying, "Behold, the dwelling place of God is with man. He will dwell with them." (Revelation 21:3)

Our expectations for Advent, remember, are two-fold. At this time of year we wait for the day to commemorate the long-expected Messiah's birth.

In a tiny town, noted primarily as the home of King David, a poor couple forced to travel for a Roman census at an awkward time in their lives, welcomes into their family an "illegitimate" baby. The shepherds are in awe. Having strained their voices telling their story all the way from the hillside, they stand quietly watching this promised One as he sleeps.

Do they remember Zechariah's words? Does Mary?

Be silent, all flesh, before the Lord, for he has roused himself from his holy dwelling. (Zechariah 2:13)

Here he is, world. The long-expected one. His second Advent is not unlike it. He will again make his dwelling among us. Among all of us.

***

Remember us, God, although we are forgetful. Show us how to live in waiting. Give us the vision of us all living together with you. Take away our narrow-mindedness and our belief in our own social structures. We pray for your light and understanding.

Amen

Reflections:

1. Do I believe in a savior for all nations? How do I need to adjust my understanding of peoples in order to see them as God sees them?
2. What does this say about our social structures and reliance on political leaders? How might Advent call me to see things differently?

December 8

Good News

If we accept this Infant as our God, then we accept our own obligation to grow with Him in a world of arrogant power and travel with Him as He ascends to Jerusalem and to the Cross, which is the denial of power.
 -Thomas Merton in Love and Living

One day, after returning to Galilee on the heels of his baptism and grueling wilderness experience, Jesus entered his hometown synagogue. Whether or not he requested a specific reading, he was given the scroll of Isaiah to read. Jesus, who does everything intentionally, opened to what we know as Isaiah 61. His experience in the wilderness was Spirit-led and Satan-attended. It was a period of reflection, prayer, and starvation. He had not yet named his apostles, his mother still relied on him, and he had not yet had the opportunity to plan out how he was to live out this special mission, which he was called to accomplish. It had been mere weeks since his eccentric cousin had called attention to him in the Jordan

River. "Lamb of God," was how John referred to him. "Come to take away the sins of the world." He knew how lambs took away sin. It was only through blood and death. Their own blood and death (Leviticus 17:11).

This would not be a triumphant proclamation. It would not be a ministry of conquering and celebrating. At least not by the time it all ended. He would need the strength of the Holy Spirit, his Spirit, and the approval of his Father. He had some decisions to make. Where would the boundaries be? How human would Jesus choose to be? He had emptied himself, but would he be able to maintain some of his god-reserve for the sake of success, for the sake of recognition? Wouldn't his ministry be irrelevant if no one recognized him? This is the crux of Jesus' temptations (both metaphorically and literally), and although Satan likely did not comprehend the extent of his defeat, this episode marked the initial crushing of the serpent's head. Jesus would do this on his own terms, on his Father's terms, in fact. He would fight…. like a man.

In ways the prophet could never know, Isaiah wrote words to the nation of Israel which, five hundred years later, would guide the Savior, the Immanuel, as he unrolled to this section:

> The Spirit of the Lord God is upon me,
> because the Lord has anointed me
> to bring good news to the poor;

> he has sent me to bind up the brokenhearted;
>
> to proclaim liberty to the captives,
>
> and the opening of the prison to those who are bound;
>
> to proclaim the year of the Lord's favor,
>
> and the day of vengeance of our God,
>
> to comfort all who mourn;
>
> to grant to those who mourn in Zion
>
> to give them a beautiful headdress instead of ashes,
>
> the oil of gladness instead of mourning,
>
> the garment of praise instead of a faint spirit;
>
> that they may be called oaks of righteousness,
>
> the planting of the Lord, that he may be glorified.
>
> (Isaiah 61:1-3)

These would be the hallmarks of his ministry: the poor, the afflicted, the powerless, the blind, the destitute, all receiving comfort and hope. Their mourning would be transformed to joy, not by a kingly edict or governmental overthrow, or even by gaining a political foothold. He would be an oak of righteousness, planted firmly in the earth, in the first-century earth of Galilee, and barely beyond. His people would be oaks of righteousness, and though their sphere would extend further beyond Israel's border, the "proclamation of the Lord's favor" would be so unexpected in nature.

When Jesus looked up from the scroll, he quickly realized that they had misunderstood his pronouncement. "Today, this Scripture has been fulfilled in your hearing." He knew they did not understand, because they had seemed too pleased. So, he tried again.

"Truly, I say to you, no prophet is acceptable in his hometown. But in truth, I tell you, there were many widows in Israel in the days of Elijah, when the heavens were shut up three years and six months, and a great famine came over all the land, and Elijah was sent to none of them but only to Zarephath, in the land of Sidon, to a woman who was a widow. And there were many lepers in Israel in the time of the prophet Elisha, and none of them was cleansed, but only Naaman the Syrian."
(Luke 4:24-27)

Sidon? Syria? Was he serious? There, abruptly, ended the smiles, nods, and "gracious words." He grew smaller in their eyes, yet more of a threat. It was pleasant when he proclaimed good news which rang of kingship and liberating edicts. A proclamation could have ousted the Romans, fulfilled all the hopes of Israel, made Israel the great, chosen nation again. They had enjoyed the thought that healing and preaching might have preceded a successful insurrection. However, he had ruined it when he had mentioned the northern outliers in Sidon, those despised further inland in Syria. The people had not forgotten their enemies' rapacious history. Jesus' audacity to chastise them in their own synagogue, while simultaneously approving of the morally and ethnically degenerate, was too much. These people were no examples of morality. They were unholy and undeserving of graciousness. They were not even Jewish. They were not God's people. We might even say they were un-American.

Jesus confronted the people, and he confronts us, to apply our compassion and empathy toward others outside of our comfort zone. He urges us to throw out a wider net to pull in those with God's graciousness and love.

But what does this have to do with Christmas? Why would we contemplate these thoughts and synagogue readings of an adult Jesus during a time of Advent? Although there is not a baby in a manger, or lowing cattle here, what we do have is an understanding of the incarnation: Immanuel, God is with us. Quietly fighting off the demons of pride, fear, and loneliness, Jesus fully takes on his humanity, and it will be for the duration of his ministry. He will not claim divinity as a right. He will walk in the steps of a man without looking back. Guided by the Spirit, he embodies not the typical Jewish man, but the paragon of humanity.

He is Immanuel. Jesus is one of us.

***

Dear Lord,
We want to be oaks of righteousness. Teach us to walk in your ways and rely on the Father. Teach us we are the poor, brokenhearted captives, but you have come to be just like us.

Reflections:

1. How am I bringing the good news to the poor this season?
2. Where is my compassion weakest? How can Jesus help me increase my compassion for the broken-hearted?

December 9

Word of Wonder

Our failure is not that we choose earth over heaven: it is that we fail to see the divine in the earth, already active and working, pouring forth grace and spilling glory into our lives.

-Makoto Fujimura in Silence and Beauty: Hidden Faith Born of Suffering

We fail when we try to explain his identity: one hundred percent God and one hundred percent human. It doesn't make sense, and it never truly resonates with us. We can't pretend our tidy platitude satisfies us. No explanation will suffice because he is the unexplainable. The world did not comprehend him nor was it able to thwart his purposes (John 1:5). We are wrong when we think we understand his divinity, and we are far away from grasping his humanity.

None of those who spoke and wrote of his eventual arrival fully understood; none of those who were eyewitnesses to the incarnation received the gravity of the situation. Not even the so-called Magi, or wise men, knew the heavy portent which led them onward through changing villages and terrain.

> Star of wonder,
>
> star of light,
>
> star of beauty, burning bright.

It is not the star that makes us wonder, or is wonderful itself, but it directs us. It is the wonder of what it all means. How is it possible? He is wonderful, and he creates within us an insatiable sense of wonder. How? In what way? What does it all mean? To what extent? We ask the questions that are due adverbs, but the reply is an incomprehensible noun. A Word full of all parts of speech. Of the Father. With God.

He was in the beginning with God. All things were made through him, and without him was not any thing made that was made. (John 1:2-3)

He is the subject, but he is the One whom the prepositional phrase modifies, both the pronoun and the antecedent. He is. And there is no way of diagramming him.

Uncomprehending, full of struggles and skeptical questions and wonder: this is how we live. This is how we ought to be. Faith is wonder. Faith does not depend on perfect understanding, nor does salvation mandate flawless theology. This wonder provides us with no simple answers to Jesus' identity, but it fills our lives with its transformative power, confident beyond our comprehension. We may never be satisfied with any explanation of how Christ can inhabit both natures. We may always argue with one another over the extent to which the Messiah is eternal and divine, or ephemeral and created. However, his essence never depends on our belief, nor his unmerited love on our proper Christology.

Star of wonder, guide us to his heavenly light.

***

Holy Word,

You are marvelous and wonderful. We thank you and praise you for creating this world of trees and rivers, of friendships and feasts for us. We ask you to give us the wonder and appreciation of children. Let us never grow weary of watching icy flakes softly falling or discovering new ways you guide us. We admit we never fully comprehend you, but let us walk closer, trusting in your truth, goodness and beauty. Amen.

Reflections:

1. What is my favorite way to think about Jesus' divinity and humanity?
2. What is the relationship between faith and understanding? Which one comes first? Which one is more important?

December 10

Light

The incarnate Word is with us, is still speaking, is present always, yet leaves no sign but everything that is.
    -Wendell Berry in Sabbath Poems

All faults are the same. There is only one fault: incapacity to feed upon light, for where capacity to do this has been lost all faults are possible...There is no good apart from this capacity.
    -Simone Weil in Gravity and Grace

Thousands of years ago, when an ancient man of the Hebrews, inspired by the Holy Spirit, first set out to record an account of creation, he described the world as "formless" and "void." God's first words were, "Let there be light." From the moment light burst upon the scene, it differentiated the darkness, and he deemed its illuminating quality to be good.

God called the light Day, and the darkness he called Night. And there was evening and there was morning, the first day. (Genesis 1:5)

Genesis opens with God creating light, and thousands of years later, the Gospel according to John also opens with light. The light of the world bends down and pitches his tent in our camp. The light is one of us.

The Word became flesh and dwelt among us, and we have seen his glory, glory as of the only Son from the Father, full of grace and truth. (John 1:14)

Not only did the incarnate Word arrive when we were in the dark, but he came when we had not even realized that we had always been swallowed up in the darkness. We had forgotten the light; we had grown accustomed to our myopia and blurry vision. We saw dimness as normal, as if there was no more to be expected.

Then, Jesus arrived, first wrinkled and helpless, swaddled in the cloth strips of a despised townspeople, and later speaking grace and truth. His morality didn't stun anyone. There were plenty of good, law-abiding Jews around. Although he seemed curious and bright, Jerusalem and the surrounding towns had their fill of priests and scholars quoting statutes and moral codes at them. They had received the words of the prophets with rigid interpretations. Instead, the people followed Jesus for his kindness, his stories, for the potentiality of healing the sick and the hopeless. When he spoke to you, his arm rested on your shoulder. He wasn't afraid to touch the leper, speak to the Greek, face the crowds, enter the homes of the disreputable or play with the neighbor's daughter. Light came from his eyes and illuminated the poor in spirit but blinded those who believed in the wealth of their goodness.

His light was for all who recognized its life. He would draw us to himself, but not everyone accepted its allure. He illuminated the world, his own creation, so we could see one another clearly. Some insisted they were good enough. They believed their actions did not shroud them in darkness, but that they merely tripped on occasion in a dim light. They righted themselves and went on, not understanding their actions were only a symptom. The darkness was in their heart. Meanwhile, the Word cried out with the primordial words of creation, "Let there be light."

Some despaired there would always be darkness, fearing the light would never be strong enough to penetrate the sadness, the evil, the pettiness, the intolerance, the hatred and the exclusivity. However, he did not come to show them light, but instead said, "I am the light of the world" (John 8:12). As they marveled at his presence among them, they were further stunned by his following pronouncement.

"You are light of the world.... let your light shine before others, so that they may see your good works and give glory to your Father who is in heaven." (Matthew 5:14, 16)

***

Dear Incarnate Word,

Teach us to trust in your truth, goodness, and beauty. Nourish us by your eternal light. We pray that as you show us the way, we can enlighten the paths of others.

Jesus, in your name we pray,

Amen

Reflections:

1. What does it mean to reflect the light of Christ in my life?
2. Where do I see the most darkness? How can I help?

December 11

Once Before Time

God became what we are so we could become what he is.
    -Athanasius of Alexandria in On the Incarnation of the Word

The virgin birth has never been a major stumbling block in my struggle with Christianity; it's far less mind-boggling than the Power of all Creation stooping so low as to become one of us.
    -Madeleine L'Engle, from A Stone for a Pillow

Once before time, he hung up all the stars, he was one of the three unified personalities who held back rushing waters from the firmament, and in human time, toppled the wheels and chariots and horses of the world's greatest empire of the time, and sent them drowning in the Red Sea by a strong east wind. Once before time, he created wondrous spiritual beings who served him and delivered messages, and in human time reversed death for three faithful men in a fiery furnace. Now, he rests, almost helplessly in swaddling clothes, dressed by a teenaged girl, nearly helpless herself in an occupied region and within a society where few would believe her, but still fiercely determined to do what is right. He came to a particular time and place, to a particular people. Born into a family devoutly following Torah, he lay squirming in the feeding trough under the loving gaze of his young mother. The great I AM had become part of the head count for Caesar Augustus. For Mary, he was a treasure and a worrisome responsibility. For the Romans he would be an extra tax, then later, a problem which would grow more and more taxing. He was first-born son, secretly adopted. He was wrinkled legs and colicky cry. He was the Word become flesh. He was "God has not abandoned us."

For Joseph, he was a mystery and a command.

But as he considered these things, behold, an angel of the Lord appeared to him in a dream, saying, "Joseph, son of David, do not fear to take Mary home as your wife, for that which is conceived in her is from the Holy Spirit. She will bear a son, and you shall call his name Jesus, for he will save his people from their sins." (Matthew 1:20-21)

Jesus, son of Joseph, son of David, who had once been, who still is, God. He has come.

All this took place to fulfill what the Lord had spoken by the prophet: "Behold, the virgin shall conceive and bear a son, and they shall call his name Immanuel" (which means, God with us). (Matthew 1:22-23)

Great is his love and certain his coming. God held such a great love for us that he chose to bridge the divide himself. He came as one of us. God stretched down from heaven and pouring himself out, bridged heaven and earth. How is this olive-skinned newborn a salvation? How is he God with us? He is.

"No one has ever gone into heaven except he who descended from heaven, the Son of Man." (John 3:13)

If God is among us, then in this way, it is possible for us to be with God. Only through Immanuel can we do this. Here, we are reminded of Jesus' words as a young man at night speaking to a significant teacher of the law.

"No one has ever gone into heaven…"

Here we are reminded of Jesus' baptism with the Spirit alighting on his shoulder, Elijah being whisked up to heaven in a fiery chariot, and Jacob's vision of angels ascending and descending the ladder. Yet these were not enough. God said, I want to walk with them again. So, God, through the substantive flesh of Jesus, opened a spectacular trail to himself.

Advent means he is coming. Advent means we are his. Immanuel. God has come to be one of us.

***

Immanuel,

Jesus, you are God with us. We are amazed that your love never has waned for us. We bow in humility and sorrow that we have moved so far away from you. Son of God, we look to you, thankful that you have come. Walk with us, God. Let us walk again with you.
Amen.

Reflections:
1. Which part of the gospel seems the most fantastic and difficult for me to believe?
2. What has been the most difficult thing God has led me to do?

December 12

Let It Be

> *Him whom the heavens cannot*
> *contain, the womb of one woman*
> *bore, She ruled our Ruler; she carried*
> *Him in whom we are; she gave milk*
> *to our Bread.*
>
> —Augustine of Hippo from Sermon 184

And here I have lamely related to you the uneventful chronicle of two foolish children in a flat who most unwisely sacrificed for each other the greatest treasure of their house. But in a last word to the wise of these days let it be said that of all who give gifts these two were the wisest. Of all who give and receive gifts, such as they are wisest. Everywhere they are wisest. They are the magi.

—O. Henry in "The Gift of the Magi"

From the beginning Mary shows herself to be much like us, and exceptional at the same time. Upon hearing words of comfort and encouragement, she is instantly worried about the greeting. Perhaps she never comprehended the words of assurance but was only stunned by an angel interrupting the monotony of her daily chores.

"Greetings, O favored one, the Lord is with you!" (Luke 1:28)

How often do we react with suspicion to goodness and warm-heartedness? How many times do we look over our shoulder expecting to see someone else receiving the accolades? Although Mary grew up in a pious home, she was not likely waiting with bated breath for the culmination of the prophets to appear in actuality that day. How often do we pray fervently in hope, never acknowledging answered prayer simply because we do not perceive it? How many times have we been shocked into realizing that for which we wore the Father out for years has, at last, been granted? We live in hope and are then stupefied when we receive what we have sought.

The angel, who had yet to reveal himself to her, reassured her.

"Do not be afraid, Mary, for you have found favor with God." (Luke 1:30)

God was pleased with her. Already her young life had been characterized by devotion. Just as the Lord had noticed the heart of

Noah, and Job, and Abraham, and Hannah and David, so God looked on Mary and was pleased. This humble girl had had no opportunity to distinguish herself in life, nor would she likely ever in the world's estimation. Yet God looked down and approved. A grave and wonderful task was laid at her feet.

"And behold, you will conceive in your womb and bear a son, and you shall call his name Jesus. He will be great and will be called the Son of the Most High. And the Lord God will give to him the throne of his father David, and he will reign over the house of Jacob forever, and of his kingdom there will be no end." (Luke 1:31-33)

Mary may have remembered the words of Isaiah the prophet, of Micah, of Zechariah, of Moses. She, like the rest of her family and village, had been awaiting a Messiah. Did awaiting mean always tomorrow, always next year? Was the Advent forever to be expected in some far-off date, a coming of unlikelihood? Here, in her hometown, an angel had appeared with such fantastic news of Messiahship and salvation, of kingly generosity and eternity.

The Lord's generosity overflows not only to this young girl, but to her nation of people who have become neglected, oppressed, and controlled. In a patriarchal society, Mary is given the honor of birthing God into the world free of male initiative. In a single greeting, Mary receives word that the Lord has not forgotten, or abandoned them. She is generous in return, holding back nothing of who she is and the little she has to offer. Is it easier to give when you have little to hand over?

Mary, in her humility, simplicity and generosity, asks a question similar to some of her predecessors of faith. Even in our utmost trust we feel the need for explanation. "How will this be, since I am a virgin?" (Luke 1:34)

Abraham, the father of the nation, questions, "Shall a child be born to a man who is a hundred years old?" (Genesis 17:17)

Moses, in front of a burning bush, answers God incredulously and fearfully, "Who am I that I should go to Pharaoh and bring the children of Israel out of Egypt?" (Exodus 3:11)

The Lord introduces himself to the patriarchs through visions and audible speech, and to Moses he reveals himself in the flames of a wilderness shrub.

And he said, "I am the God of your father, the God of Abraham, the God of Israel, and the God of Jacob." (Exodus 3:6)

While the Lord speaks directly with Abraham and Moses, he entrusts his messenger Gabriel to reveal his purpose to Mary. Here in the angelic greeting, we have echoes of the Lord showing himself to Moses at Horeb. Both Moses and Mary are privy to the Lord introducing himself as the Deliverer.

At the onset of Luke's gospel account, we hear angelic introduction of the description of God. He is powerful and he is trinitarian by nature. While Gabriel relays the Lord's message, he also relays how all three personalities of God—Father, Son and Holy Spirit—are intricately involved in the incarnation.

"And behold, you will conceive in your womb and bear a son, and you shall call his name Jesus. He will be great and will be called the Son of the Most High…. The Holy Spirit will come upon you, and the power of the Most High will overshadow you; therefore the child to be born will be called holy—the Son of God." (Luke 1:31-32, 35)

Mary's faithfulness demonstrates how God longs to fill us with his power. Would we have chosen as God did? To whom would we have entrusted the rearing and teaching of the "Son of the Most High?" Mary proves her mettle when she hears of God's generosity and graciousness to her and to her older cousin Elizabeth. As she submitted to God within her, she had already welcomed him within her heart.

And Mary said, "Behold, I am the servant of the Lord; let it be to me according to your word." And the angel departed from her. (Luke 1:38)

This "let it be" is often described, as Ignatius named it, a holy indifference. Ignatius did not mean apathy, but rather a holy and humble attitude to allow God to use her in the way he chooses for his purposes. In these words to Gabriel, and to her God, she allowed the Holy Spirit to lead her in ways she never would have dreamt or chosen for herself. "Let it be" meant she surrendered any girlish dreams of happy, carefree betrothals and respectable reputations. None of her questions were answered, no more fears relieved, but Mary knew God's character to be good, and she trusted in his name implicitly. Her son, Spirit and flesh, would be Jesus, the Lord saves. He would save her from the dangers of childbirth, and he would save her people from their sins, drawing them all back to the Most High God.

"Let it be to me according to your word."

As Augustine says, "She gave milk to our Bread."

As Jesus grew, she taught him to walk with "bands of love." She held his hand and led him to the fields, she may have checked on him in Joseph's workshop. Did she whisper a psalm to him in the evening with a kiss on the forehead? Over time, as she tucked her God-son in bed at night, she may have taught him to repeat his own holy prayer of indifference. Later, in a garden, at the most difficult time in his life, Jesus lifted up a similar prayer.

"Father, if you are willing, remove this cup from me. Nevertheless, not my will, but yours, be done." (Luke 22:42)

"Let it be…"

***

Lord and Savior,

What difficult words! How can we ever submit so fully to you? Forgive our reluctance and lack of faith. Forgive our stubbornness and refusal to follow your Spirit. Teach us Mary's words in our own lives. Where would you like us to go? What would you like us to do? Good, good God help us to trust completely in your love for us. Let it be as you have said.

Amen.

Reflections:

1. Is there something in my life now that seems impossible? Can I trust God?
2. What might I need to relinquish? In what way do I need to submit or turn things over to God?

December 13

They Made Known the Saying

Love recognizes no barriers. It jumps hurdles, leaps fences, penetrates walls to arrive at its destination full of hope.
    -Maya Angelou from her Facebook on January 11, 2013

While shepherds kept their watching
o'er silent flocks by night,
behold throughout the heavens
there shone a holy light.
    Go, tell it on the mountain,
    over the hills and everywhere;
    go, tell it on the mountain
    that Jesus Christ is born.
    -collected by John Wesley Work, Jr., from the African American spiritual and carol

He is holy, and we are sinful. He is divine, and we are destitute. He is mighty, and we are helpless. He is full of love, and we are bereft. It is in these truths we discover both the bad news and the good news intertwined. Herein lies the Gospel. Jesus came leaping hurdles, breaking walls, destroying barriers to be one of us, to rescue us, to be near us. He came in poverty, abandoning the peace and splendor of heaven, the omniscience and communion of deity, and chose an adopted family without means or influence.

He is one of us because he loves us.

It is good news that God has come down. And that is exactly how the shepherds heard it. Perhaps they were initially frightened, maybe stunned that of all people simple herdsmen were among the first privy to such a glorious announcement. Someone special had been born who had come to rescue them, a Savior! There was not time for reflection. The shepherds ran for Bethlehem to find this good news for themselves. What did they even do with their flocks?

When the angels went away from them into heaven, the shepherds said to one another, "Let us go over to Bethlehem and see this thing that has happened, which the Lord has made known to us." And they went with haste and found Mary and Joseph, and the baby lying in a manger. And when they saw it, they made known the saying that had been told them concerning this child. And all who heard it wondered at what the shepherds told them. (Luke 2:15-18)

Did they choose their words carefully? Did they all talk at once? Did they even know where to begin? Were they grabbing people by the shoulders as they passed by? Did they smile?

How do we share good news? Is it evident on our faces? Is there always a catch in our voice or a sense of awe and wonder?

The shepherds made known the saying about the Christ-child. Did they get some facts wrong? Were they even sure what to expect? With "Glory to God in the highest and on earth peace among those with whom he is pleased!" (Luke 2:14) still ringing in their ears, the shepherds spread the word. After that day, many in Bethlehem knew something had happened, something they couldn't ignore. There were shepherds laughing.

This Advent, how can we make known the saying? There are many who hurt and are lonely and numb. Perhaps we are one of them. It is a joyful message. It is good news: a Savior has been born. Advent is not the season to quarrel or point out differences. It is not the time to hold on to grudges or bitter thoughts. We do not discriminate between shepherds and kings, for the One who has come is certainly both.

This Advent let's praise God and spread the word along with the shepherds. He has come. Immanuel!

> How beautiful upon the mountains
> are the feet of him who brings good news,
> who publishes peace, who brings

good news of happiness,

who publishes salvation,

who says to Zion, "Your God reigns." (Isaiah 52:7)

***

Glory and honor to you, God, for this is joyful news! Give us a sense of our need for your coming and respond with pure joy and wonder like the shepherds. May our enthusiasm bubble over and help us to make known in our towns and neighborhoods the beautiful truth that you have come.

Reflections:

1. Why is Jesus' birth such good news?
2. What is my favorite way to talk about Jesus?

December 14

Remembering

The past is prophetic in that it asserts loudly that wars are poor chisels for carving out peaceful tomorrows.
 -Martin Luther King, Jr. from his speech on February 25, 1967 "The Casualties of the War in Vietnam"

Bet on the baby and listen to the clock ticking away.
 -Walter Brueggeman in Celebrating Abundance

Peace. It was what the shepherds relayed in their message to all whom they stopped en route to Bethlehem. It must have been a terrifying peace spoken from the mouths of winged bursts of light. Though terror gripped their hearts, joyful peace sent them racing into the nearby village, remembering their celestial experience to all who would hear. Finally, the young mother listened, taking in the peculiar words of these rugged men smelling of meadow and sheep, sweat and the last bite of a stale lunch. Mary surely remembered their visit on the night her firstborn came into the world. She may have remembered their breathless entrance, or their awkward stance at the edge of the room, mouths agape, yet eyes still shining from the angelic news.

But Mary treasured up all these things, pondering them in her heart. (Luke 2:19)

She had remembered with her cousin Elizabeth. Though too old for conceiving, she had, indeed, conceived. Mary had taken comfort in family and hidden safety where few people knew her story or recognized her face. Quickly approaching Elizabeth, she remembered family connections and moments of warmth and happy work in community. Elizabeth's greeting filled her with the joy of assurance. What did she remember? Evidently, it was the blessings of the Lord, his constant care, his love for the poor and unfortunate, and his promises dating back to Abraham through the present.
"My soul magnifies the Lord,
   and my spirit rejoices in God my Savior,
for he has looked on the humble estate of his servant.
   For behold, from now on all generations will call me blessed;
for he who is mighty has done great things for me,
   and holy is his name.
And his mercy is for those who fear him
   from generation to generation.

He has shown strength with his arm;
> he has scattered the proud in the thoughts of their hearts;

he has brought down the mighty from their thrones
> and exalted those of humble estate;

he has filled the hungry with good things,
> and the rich he has sent away empty.

He has helped his servant Israel,
> in remembrance of his mercy,

as he spoke to our fathers,
> to Abraham and to his offspring forever." (Luke 1:46-56)

What was it exactly that she remembered? The fontanelle of her baby's head? The crowded outer room of the house mere hours after giving birth? Her own encounter with an angel, more personal and intimate, but no less startling? Why did she remember and treasure these things? Because this baby was for the salvation of the world, and she needed to get it right. Because the shame and potential rejection of raising a boy whom many assumed to be from dubious circumstances would be difficult. Remembering would be an anchor. It would tether her and strengthen her when society looked askance or whispered behind her back. Because every mother remembers and treasures those first moments and days and months of motherhood. They would serve both to comfort her and pierce her heart years later. Remembering God's mercy and faithfulness and promise brought hope for the future. In short, Mary remembered the character of God.

Eight days after the birth of Jesus the family was in Jerusalem entering the temple. There would be more things to treasure and remember and ponder. Joseph remembered the law. "Every male who first opens the womb shall be holy to the Lord" (Luke 2:23). Although this was no son of Joseph, still he remembered. Remembering is honoring and obeying our way into a trusting relationship.

The couple was approached by a man who remembered a promise. He held Jesus, praising God and called him his "salvation" (Luke 2:30) and "a light for revelation to the Gentiles" (Luke 2:32) How can you not remember such things?

An old woman appeared. She seemed to live in the temple. When she also spoke of the "redemption of Jerusalem" (Luke 2:38), she was looking back, remembering as a prophet all the prophets who had been before her. They had spanned centuries in the past, but always looked ahead. She could scarcely remember the scent of her husband or the bridge of his nose. He had been gone so long. She had lived without him now for decades, yet she remembered the word of the Lord. And now it was here before her, and Anna blessed this young girl, barely a woman. Mary would surely remember this, yet full of wonder regarding this "redemption" and "salvation."

Over thirty years later this baby would rise up from the beginnings of a meal and remember something. During the meal which commemorated freedom from slavery, he would perform the task of a slave, and remember when he performed wondrous acts of creation. He would remember one of his friends would soon be leaving, and he wouldn't be able to stop him, and he remembered the entire plan he had signed up for. It was a violent plan, a literally excruciating plan, a plan borne of love and mercy. He remembered a plan of redemption.

He began to serve the bread, the symbolic staple of life, broke it and said, "Remember me." He lifted his cup of wine, referencing his own blood, and repeated his request: "Remember me." Why does he ask us to remember him? Was he pleading for sentimentality, hoping his friends would not forget him? It was not for the sake of nostalgia that he commanded remembrance. It was a watchfulness for the future. It was for the sake of his friends, and for us.

Remembering should not bind us to days gone by or limit us to always looking back in time where we can never return. It does not glamorize our past, nor gloss over old memories. Rather, remembering has a purpose tied to hopefulness for the things to come. It is for the growing and careful cultivating of faith. Mary remembered the shepherds, for she knew she was tasked with raising up the good Shepherd. Joseph remembered the law of the Lord, even at his adopted son's circumcision, because he knew one day this infant would fulfill the law. Anna and Simeon remembered the gracious promises of the Holy Spirit, for although they would never see its completion with their own eyes, they looked far beyond it to see the salvation and redemption of all the nations.

We remember with bread and wine, with Christmas and presents and Advent candles, and with acts of love, because we, like

Mary, have seen the character of God. Only because we look back and remember God's graciousness, Jesus' faithfulness, and the Spirit's mercifulness, can we look ahead hopefully and with great peace.

***

Lord,

Grant us the gift of remembering and remembering rightly. Help us to move past the temptation to glorify the past, but to trust in your faithful character. Help us to remember all your mercies, and to remember them to our friends, our children and to all whom you love. Work through us to bring about your peace to the world. Amen.

Reflections:

1. What do I frequently remember during this Advent season?
2. What am I looking forward to the most at Jesus' final Advent?

December 15

The Incarnation in Suffering

Sins couldn't be laundered by good results.
    -Min Jin Lee from Pachinko

The tragedy is not that things are broken. The tragedy is that they are not mended again.
    -Alan Paton from Cry, the Beloved Country

It will not be so in the Mended Wood.
    -S. D. Smith from Ember Falls (The Green Ember #2)

There is irony in Luke's account of the angels' visitation to the shepherds with their choral message of peace and good news. When the divine touched down on earth to save it, there was no immediate eradication of sin, violence or injustice. Instead, they seemed to be exacerbated. The darkness did not understand this peasant girl's "bastard," new-born son was the eternal light, the light of the world, for the world.

There is a grave irony in this child entering the world of the Pax Romana. The great Roman peace would eventually be unwilling to protect him and would be culpable for his execution. Even shortly before his birth, Rome could not maintain the peace of its citizens in the outlying Jewish districts.

The birth of Jesus gripped King Herod the Great with fear. Here, in this helpless baby from Galilean parents, was a threat like no other he had experienced in his political career. The prophecies, though intangible, heightened his paranoia. Having already done away with his wife and numerous other family members, Herod met his problems head on.

Then Herod, when he saw that he had been tricked by the wise men, became furious, and he sent and killed all the male children in Bethlehem and in all that region who were two years old or under, according to the time that he had ascertained from the wise men. Then was fulfilled what was spoken by the prophet Jeremiah:

> "A voice was heard in Ramah,
> weeping and loud lamentation,
> Rachel weeping for her children;
> she refused to be comforted,
>   because they are no more." (Matthew 2:16-18)

Why would God introduce his Son into the world in such a way? Why should there be the slaughter of innocents succeeding glad tidings of peace to all humanity? A mother who watched as her toddler is impaled, and flung to the side, would have a difficult time hearing the angelic herald:

"Glory to God in the highest,
and on earth peace among
those with whom he is pleased!" (Luke 2:14)

Still, today, the world reels with the pain and confusion of suffering and injustice. It is often the innocent who suffer. As we suffer, or watch others suffer, we question why God does not intervene. We doubt his love, his justice, or his ability to protect us from the evil of the imperfect world in which we are trapped. This is not the first time in the text that other innocents have perished for the sake of the deliverer. As the Israelites cried out to Jehovah for salvation from the Egyptian bondage, God answers their cries. However, he answers them much later, four hundred years later than they expected, and not before hundreds of enslaved baby boys were left exposed to die, or be impaled, strangled, or dumped into the Nile River. With the death of Christ, the One died for the many. At the birth of Moses and Jesus, however, many died for the one.

It is like this today. Empires, and powers-that-be, will always engage in acts of self-preserving violence. At some point, the government or empire that God has ordained, will step out to be a god itself. Invariably, if questioned, power will react with oppression or violence. Empire claims God until God is the enemy. When power is threatened, ego lashes out in ugly ways. Public service lasts only until God himself is perceived as the threatening enemy. Empire acts from self-preservation, fear and bondage to absolute power. God always acts out of freedom and with love. It is not God who slaughters for the sake of his messenger, but empire.

> When Herod the king heard this, he was troubled, and all Jerusalem with him…. (Matthew 2:3)

Can we, in the twenty-first century, imagine in the United States of America or in other powerful, democratic Western nations, a tyrant's paranoia and fear infecting an entire city? Would an entire nation of people succumb to fear and bigotry simply at the prospect of someone or something destroying their way of life, their global prestige? Nations and empires have always been in the business of excluding others, frequently through dishonorable, or even violent, means. Yet God is determined to include us all: Magi and Jewish scholars, small town peasants and turncoat peddlers, sixth generation church members and struggling immigrants barely getting by.

The good news for us today, whether we are in the United States or modern-day Egypt, France or Uzbekistan, is that we do not have to make sense of fragile but powerful egos, nor monolithic political systems and religions. Matthew's gospel tells us that some misguided but gentle wise men came from the East to meet a new king. Some historians believe them to be of the early monotheistic Zoroastrians. The crazed Herod, part Jewish, part Gentile sell-out to the Roman empire, offered little moral guidance. There is no proof which indicates the "right" religions are based on superior morality alone. If morality was the world's salvation, we could all pick our favorite moral system, and the world could certainly be a better place. Only God is good, however. No, Jesus did not invade legal systems and political regimes in order to make us moral. He came to obliterate death and to elongate the bridge over sin and to unite us back with God.

So, there is no violence that will end our suffering. There is no oppression which will broker peace. We might be able to bandy about terms like "peace-keepers," "preemptive strikes," "casualties of war," or worse, "collateral damage," in order to desensitize ourselves to the fact that we are bowing down to the idol of stability and empire. We might say the ends don't always justify the means. Novelist Min Jin Lee, rather, says sins can't be "laundered by good results." Dirty is dirty, and our world of empire with some God poured on top has grown filthy.

Matthew's gospel, in contrast to Luke's, shows us the uncomfortable side of Christmas. After we wait through Advent, we are shocked when it isn't all sweet and joyful. Much of Advent deals in oppression and injustice, and even death. For when the divine intersects with a hurting, blinded world, there will always be adverse reactions. Let us live, then, sighted, for a different world.

Christ came as Immanuel to embrace humanity. He came to be like us, so that God could re-create us like him. Christ did not come to topple tyrants and dictators. We are still left to live in the midst of them—for now. Rather, he came to walk about with us, work in our cubicle, be treated unjustly and to demonstrate acceptance in unforgiving, unaccepting regimes that insist on maintaining a firm grip on their power. Jesus came to demonstrate love, and to reveal the truth of his eternally established kingdom.

The story of Jesus' birth goes from bad to worse, but Immanuel did not intersect the divine with the human for such shadowy reasons. Jesus meets us at the worst of times and ushers in a new way of being and a new way of waiting. Instead, Matthew insists that this is God's story, and that regardless of how it appears now, he is the One for whom we are waiting. It is his Advent that gathers us about the evening candles, and they are his promises we cling to when the world seems overcome with the brutality and fear of empire.

***

Just and righteous God,

Although our empires cry out for violence, we long to live in the goodness of your peace. Instead of lashing out in fear, grant us patience that your righteousness will prevail. Grant us tolerance and compassion in this time of suspicion and intolerance. We pray for the Magi around us that you will protect their journey and that you will work through us to be channels of Christmas grace and peace for those who seek you. Give us courage to stand against imperial power, knowing that all truth is your truth, and all power belongs to you, oh good God!
Amen.

Reflections:

1. What injustices do I need to pray about? What can I do to bring about more of God's justice and righteousness?
2. Whom do I know is hurt and afraid? How can I listen to their fears? How can I offer words of hope?

December 16

The Holy Immigrant

Our patriotism comes straight from the Romans....The Romans really were an atheistic and idolatrous people; not idolatrous with regard to images made of stone or bronze, but idolatrous with regard to themselves. It is this idolatry of self which they have bequeathed to us in the form of patriotism.

-Simone Weil in The Need for Roots: Prelude to a Declaration of Duties Towards Mankind

In the midst of the murderous chaos, Jesus quietly slipped out of the country with his family. God's hand protected him and guided him to safety. God did not rid the world of violence before Jesus was born, but instead, safely led his son to Egypt as the foreigner. Because of his divinity, Jesus is already a foreigner, an outsider in a world that was truly his own. Yet, however long he lived in Egypt with Mary and Joseph, he lived there as an outlier, not quite fitting in, returning only at the death of a king. In Egypt he sought asylum; returning to Galilee, he sought a home.

"Out of Egypt I called my son" (Matthew 2:15). Matthew applies the prophet Hosea's words in a peculiar way to Jesus. Indubitably, God called Jesus out of Egypt to grow up in tiny Nazareth, preparing him to take on his mission. He called him out of Egypt through the dreams of Joseph, his substitute father. Hundreds and hundreds of years prior another Joseph dreamed inspired visions of deliverance and protection. Another Joseph, from ancient times, had dreams of sibling rivalry, and dreamt of leaving his homeland. He dreamt of delivering nations, but also of family security and flourishing peoples.

Joseph led Mary and her newborn son out of harm's way, according to the Lord's direction. They were holy immigrants, fleeing one empire for another. Joseph and Mary leaned into the fantastic ways God called them. They trusted in God's salvific hand. They learned they could not trust the power of empire, but they relied on the Lord of all empires. Herod would make decisions based on greed, and fear, and panic. God delivered them out of generosity, and love, and surety.

Matthew uses Hosea's original text in a beautiful way, allowing God's many layers of truth to be revealed. God delivers the nation of Israel from the bonds of Egypt, and God rescues his son Jesus from the clutches of Herod. While Hosea is reminding Israel of their past in bondage and their formation as a nation, he is also, perhaps unwittingly, speaking to the reader of the distant future, reminding us that God's hand creates, forms, delivers, and upholds. Hosea speaks the story of the great exodus as a defining moment in Israelite history, and a continuing metaphor illustrating the eternal truth: The Lord saves, not empire.

Joseph and Mary fled to Egypt with Jesus because they could not trust in the power of the Roman Empire, but at first opportunity, they also abandoned Egypt, for the Lord revealed to them that there are no kingdoms beside his. When the Lord is with us, or more precisely, when we are with the Lord, there is hope and assurance.

When Jesus returns to his native soil with his parents, we also learn that we cannot rely on our own perception of the powerless. We are duped into believing in the greatness of power. We spurn and despise weakness and need. We fear it. We grow suspicious of it and attribute all kinds of ill motives to it. As the holy immigrants returned from the idolatrous mega-empire, they likely appeared beaten, destitute, foreign, unfamiliar, needy, and undesirable. Where should they go? Jerusalem would not welcome them. The great powers-that-be threatened if they returned to their native village, and so, Jesus, son of Heaven, settled into obscurity and unimpressive provinciality. It would seem God is not impressed by might or power, clout or leverage.

If part of the story of Advent includes the journey of refugees, what does that tell us of God? For whom are we waiting? For a great king of power? Advent is not about wielding power but about appearing lonely and tired, yet safely at the end of a trip. It is about appearing where the animals are fed, about being cradled within willing arms.

Advent is about completing a journey from strange land to dangerous familiarity because God so requested.

How does imagining Christ's return from Egypt as an immigrant family help me to appreciate the Advent season? What is my response today? I set aside nationality and concerns for the power of empire, and I see not as an American, not through the eyes of a national identity, but through faithful eyes, expectantly waiting for the promised One to come. We take up our moral responsibility based on our Advent hope of the Christ to come. At Advent, and always, we extend grace, love, and compassion to the foreigner, the powerless, or the needy and lonely. At Advent we transform into ambassadors opening our hearts to those Christ gives us (II Corinthians 5:20-21). As he crossed borders with his family, Jesus calls us to act righteously. His righteousness, also named justice, is too unwieldy for us to fit into, but he drapes it over us for the time being that we may grow into it through loving practice.

> When Israel was a child, I loved him,
> and out of Egypt I called my son.
> The more they were called,
> the more they went away;
> they kept sacrificing to the Baals
> and burning offerings to idols.
> Yet it was I who taught Ephraim to walk;
> I took them up by their arms,
> but they did not know that I healed them.

> I led them with cords of kindness,
>
> with the bands of love,
>
> and I became to them as one who eases the yoke on their jaws,
>
> and I bent down to them and fed them.
>
> (Hosea 11:1-5)

How does the prophet imagine such a God? While genocide, hatred and bigoted fear reign, God is imagined as tender, faithful, gentle, loving. He is a father nurturing a very young child. He leads with "cords of kindness." He teaches and heals them as they are learning to walk. Likewise, those who were called out, are intended to pattern this same, gentle walk.

As the Son grew up, Jesus never asked anyone to prove themselves before approaching him, nor did he withhold compassion based on one's morality, national identity, political stance, or ethnicity. Because of Advent, we set aside what it feels like to see someone through the eyes of our nationality. Never again do we gauge someone according to the empire that would claim us. We see God's truth clearly in Jesus' interaction with the tax collector Zacchaeus (Luke 19:1-10), and in his eagerness to mix with the Samaritans (John 4:1-12), the Roman centurion (Matthew 8:5-13), and some proselytized Greeks (John 12:20). At Advent we embrace those in need because we await the only One who can fill them. We recognize that empire provides false security and increases division and suspicion. However, we can reduce fear-driven responses by listening and speaking measured words of kindness. We can demonstrate the grace and love of the Creator as we uphold the highest good to "love one another" (I John 4:7).

As we imagine the holy immigrants seeking shelter at the birth of their son, or as we commemorate their return journey to Nazareth as home, we imagine a compassion for others which would not have been possible otherwise.

"Out of Egypt I called my son."

Jesus hears the continuing gentleness and grace of his Father in the prophet's words. He knows those words, that gentleness, that grace is for him also, and he repeats it, so we might do the same.

When [Jesus] saw the crowds, he had compassion for them, because they were harassed and helpless, like sheep without a shepherd. Then he said to his disciples," The harvest is plentiful, but the laborers are few; therefore, pray earnestly to the Lord of the harvest to send out laborers into his harvest. (Matthew 9:36-38)

Praise his graciousness and love, for he did not react to their sin! He did not grumble and judge why they had dragged their children along with them in the hot sun. He did not look askance at those who were not morally upright, nor at their refusal to follow the Law. Jesus did not push away those from less skilled backgrounds or rural areas. He himself was among them. He had not forgotten Egypt. He did not harshly accuse them of only wanting handouts or reject them because some wanted the Roman authorities to take care of them. He had compassion. Jesus did not come as an emissary of justice alone, but even more, as an emissary of mercy. If our Creator spoke truth and the world into existence by a mere word, as his creation may we use our words to call out truth as well. Can we see others as individuals, or do we insist on judging them based on appearance and labels? Do we dare to speak words of affirmation, proclaiming the beauty that could be called into creation if we follow it? Christ would have us call out words of compassion, inclusion, acceptance, forgiveness, and hope.

We are the sheep in Jesus' simile. We are without a shepherd. We are sick, and desperate, and in need of mercy. If we throw off the hubris of nationalism, we might see ourselves in the throng of people searching. And if we can place ourselves among them as Jesus did, then we are far more likely to be called to compassion and see in them what Jesus sees in all of us.

***

God, forgive us when we view others solely through the eyes of nationality or race. Create in us a gentle spirit, not full of fear and timidity, but full of Jesus' power and love and discipline (II Timothy 1:7). At Advent and always, may our visceral reaction consistently be to extend a hand to others. And may we all look first to love.

Reflections:

1. Are there ways I expect my own empire to save me? How can I further trust Jesus as Lord?
2. Who are the most vulnerable in my world right now? Am I practicing and demonstrating the Lord's justice, righteousness and compassion?

December 17

Dignity

And in the Incarnation the whole human race recovers the dignity of the image of God. Henceforth, any attack even on the least of man is an attack on Christ, who took the form of man, and in his own Person restored the image of God in all that bears a human form.... The incarnate Lord makes his followers the brothers of all mankind.
    -Dietrich Bonhoeffer in The Cost of Discipleship

There is no dichotomy between man and God's image. Whoever tortures a human being, whoever abuses a human being, whoever outrages a human being, abuses God's image.
    -Oscar Romero in The Violence of Love

Imago dei. The image of God. Throughout the centuries humanity has incorrectly perceived itself. Either we see ourselves at the center of everything, fabricating a bloated image of who we are, or we denigrate ourselves, believing ourselves to be worthless and malevolent. Either way, the focus is on who we are, but forgetting whose we are. In the beginning, God created them, male and female. The expression, imago dei, Latin for image of God, provides a glimpse of our value, and a glimpse of how God feels about those he created on the sixth day.

Then God said, "Let us make man in our image, after our likeness. And let them have dominion over the fish of the sea and over the birds of the heavens and over the livestock and over all the earth and over every creeping thing that creeps on the earth."

So God created man in his own image, in the image of God he created him; male and female he created them. (Genesis 1:26-27)

What does it mean to be made in the image of God? How are we to discern the significance of that phrase? It seems unsatisfactory to think we are even a pale manifestation of the Creator. Surely, we can't look like him. Is it our ability to reason, to think above instinctual desires; is it our capacity to love? Is it the immortal soul he placed in us? Could it be our free will or our ability to co-create and work alongside our Creator? Perhaps being made in God's image has something to do with us being social creatures, in need of community. Is the diversity of humanity a commentary on divinity? Does the multiplicity of peoples give a hint of the varied richness of God's nature?

Regardless of how we understand the imago dei, we intuit that it fills us with inherent value. Because he created us in his image, he approves of us; we have potential for good. Within our bones and muscles, somewhere firing between the synapses of our brain, God created us with dignity and loves us. Possessing this dignity from God has a few crucial implications, particular implications for this season of Advent.

First, being made in the image of God makes us valuable. We have the imprint of God upon us and bear something, albeit imperfectly, of his nature. In this way, even Jesus who originally was not human, but became so for our sake, shares this same imprint in human form.

[Jesus] is the radiance of the glory of God and the exact imprint of his nature, and he upholds the universe by the word of his power. (Hebrews 1:3)

Second, this imago dei, inscrutable as it may be, makes all humans equally valuable. If I see people as inferior or superior, I am not recognizing the God in them. There is no room for scorn, demeaning thoughts or condescension if I recognize God's own image, as well as our commonality.

Next, recognizing the divine touch in each person gives value to those who are often considered less than valuable. Who the "undesirables" are largely depends on our own biases or cultural standards, but often they are the poor, the foreigner, those tangled in addictions, or those with physical, emotional, intellectual, or developmental disabilities. No one is spiritually less, nor is there anyone who is created with less of God's image. The weak and the vulnerable are always close to God's heart. The aged and marginalized are among those whom God cherishes. As Mary beautifully sings, God has

...exalted those of humble estate;
he has filled the hungry with good things. (Luke 1:52-53)

When God created us, he proclaimed us to be good. We were not good for something, or at something, but good simply because we bear his image. Imago dei strips us free from utilitarian views of humanity. We are never valuable because of what we can or may contribute to society, but for the very reason that God has placed his spirit, his image, within us.

Lastly, Jesus has exalted the dignity of humankind and showcased the intrinsic value of all people by becoming human himself. Through his life as one of us, he demonstrates the beauty of the material world. As soon as Jesus first cried out from hunger in the arms of Mary, he dispels all misconceptions about the inferiority of the physical realms. Although we are limited, sinful, and flawed, it is not due to our physicality. Jesus says, here I am; I will show you who you were created to be: valuable, valued, beloved, worthy, full of dignity, full of imago dei. By becoming one of us, Jesus breaks down the barriers between holiness and the ordinary, between the spiritual and the earthy. God came to imbue humanity's obscurity and insignificance with meaning and holiness and dignity.

As he first appeared to a carpenter and a young girl, to shepherds on a hillside, as well as foreign travelers from the East, he claims us as his own.

For he who sanctifies and those who are sanctified all have one source. That is why he is not ashamed to call them brothers. (Hebrews 2:11)

***

Jesus, we are in awe of your willingness to become one of us. We thank you for showing us the beauty of any human life. We thank you for demonstrating what a life well lived in God's image looks like. Forgive us when we devalue others. Forgive us when we expect productivity or results from others before determining their worth. Help us to recognize your image and love in everyone we meet.

Amen.

Reflections:

1. Is it more difficult for me to see my own value to God, or the value of others? How can I rest in knowing I am loved by God?
2. What do I think it means to be created in the image of God?

December 18

God Is One of Us

The challenge for those of us who care about our faith and about a hurting world is to tell stories which will carry the words of grace and hope in their bones and sinews and not wear them like a fancy dress.

-Katherine Paterson in The Light of the World

Whereas today as Christians we may start with the assumption that Jesus is God, then marvel at the miracle of his humanity, the disciples unequivocally knew him to be human, a teacher, and friend. He was Joseph's son, a carpenter, a great storyteller. He could read the Torah. They knew his favorite dish at dinner, and the way he picked the fine bones from his teeth. They knew his scent after a long day of walking and how to read the expression on his face when he grew tired or irritated. However, they struggled through Jesus' entire ministry over his messianic identity. They grappled with his absolute divinity, because first, he was one of them.

And a great windstorm arose, and the waves were breaking into the boat, so that the boat was already filling. But [Jesus] was in the stern asleep on the cushion. And they woke him and said to him, "Teacher, do you not care that we are perishing?" And he awoke and rebuked the wind and said to the sea, "Peace! Be still!" And the wind ceased, and there was a great calm. He said to them, "Why are you so afraid? Have you still no faith?" And they were filled with great fear and said to one another, "Who then is this, that even the wind and the sea obey him?" (Mark 4:37-41)

Peter, James, John, Andrew, and Thomas were left incredulous and unsure. They knew he was kind and wise and even powerful, but this was something beyond their understanding and their faith. They had seen him heal a man with a diseased hand, they had heard him teach the law through perplexing but insightful stories. This, however, was different. This had to do with their mortality and their fear. Who is not afraid of dying? Moreover, what person can authoritatively make demands of the natural world? While Jesus' friends may have been dumbfounded by a peek into his divinity, reading this story, we may focus on his concern for those in the boat. When God was one of us, he ate and talked like us, was encumbered with the same limited body as we are, but he also suffered and grew discouraged like we do.

During the Advent season we may want to focus on a baby, gently wrapped, with a loving family around. What we might not consider is that soon they will all be fleeing for their lives, that this baby will one day be whipped and beaten, nailed to a tree, mocked and left for dead. This baby, though his birth story is sweet and miraculous, never did have an easy life.

For it was fitting that he, for whom and by whom all things exist, in bringing many sons to glory, should make the founder of their salvation perfect through suffering. (Hebrews 2:10)

But what does suffering have to do with Advent? Without the suffering, there would be no salvation. Without the birth, there is no salvific death, nor gloriously hope-filled resurrection. Jesus wasn't made perfect through suffering; he already was perfect. Rather, suffering was the final experience he went through to know what it was to be human, in all its joys and despairs. His birth told us he was a Jewish boy. His death helps us understand he is not a distant spirit. He did not merely zip on a human costume. Jesus was one of us. Advent tells us that his own love for us brought him here. His life shows us that he knows and cares what we are going through. Do you feel abandoned? So did he. Do you feel lonely? So did he. Has your friend betrayed you? So did his. Do you feel discouraged even in the midst of a cheerful, holiday Advent season? Do you feel invisible? As if your heart might break?

Yet Christ sees. He sees the wind and the great waves, and he cries to our hearts, "Peace! Be still!"

In the days of his flesh, Jesus offered up prayers and supplications, with loud cries and tears, to him who was able to save him from death, and he was heard because of his reverence. (Hebrews 5:7)

In God's remarkable appearance as a human, he gave us a precious gift: God became one of us. Because Jesus lived an ordinary life, because he endured suffering and difficulties, free of accolades and acclaim, he meets us daily in the minutiae of our lives. Our days filled with the ordinary are extraordinary because they constantly reflect his steps.

Even as we might carry around heartache or frustration this Advent season, we can have the confidence to also carry the love and compassion of Jesus. The world is hurting. We are hurting. But there is One who lived a real life, a true life so that we can say he knows our suffering.

God is one of us.

***

Dear Jesus,

You will always be our brother, because you have lived this life, too, and you have brought us to the Father. We may not know the pain of our neighbor, or understand the confusion of our relative, but help us carry your love and compassion to others. We pray the people in our life are open to hearing about your suffering and your loving grace this season.
Amen.

Reflections:

1. Where is my greatest comfort now in the humanity of Christ? What is challenging about Christ's divinity?
2. Am I uncomfortable with the paradox of Jesus' humanity and divinity? How could I pray for the Spirit to help me in my wavering faith?

December 19

Ridiculous

The incarnation is a kind of vast joke whereby the Creator of the ends of the earth comes among us in diapers...Until we too have taken the idea of the God-man seriously enough to be scandalized by it, we have not taken it as seriously as it demands to be taken.
    -Frederick Buechner in Faces of Jesus

Holy wisdom is not clear and thin like water, but thick and dark like blood.
    -C. S. Lewis in Till We Have Faces

If you heard that the Infinite, the Spirit Creator was entering into His own Art, wouldn't you look to the clouds? Wouldn't you look to the cherubim in their storms; wouldn't you expect a tornado chariot? I would, and in my defense, I think my sensibilities are good and entirely in the right place. It is God who is gauche. And thus the surprise.
    -N. D. Wilson in Notes from the Tilt-a-Whirl: Wide-Eyed Wonder in God's Spoken World

Our civilization is not unusual in that we value power, whether it is economic, political, or military power. We roll our eyes over aphorisms like "might makes right," but then we order our lives in such a way that we proclaim its truth and trust in its promise. We crave stability and homogeneity and surety, but Christ never promised us these things. The season of Advent is an expectation, but not one in which we can reason out what and how it will all happen. Advent is a time when we completely trust in God to arrive in unexpected and new and unreasonable ways. In some ways we wait for the ridiculous.

It is ridiculous to expect one man to grow up and single-handedly overthrow the mighty Roman empire. It is ridiculous to light candles for a man now dead over two-thousand years. It is ridiculous to arrange your life without plans, or a sense of what is around the next corner. We might be prone to shake our heads at the unreasonableness of our faith. How could God make demands on us that are irrational or absurd? Without giving us promises of how he will work out the details, he demands us to be peaceful, humble, submissive, compassionate, creative, and full of selfless mercy. In a world where grittiness, brash boldness, self-promotion, passion, and divisiveness are not only the norm but perceived virtues, we can see God as unreasonable.

When God performs the ridiculous, or demands the unreasonable, he is acting out of his essence: out of love. And his love seems irrational. He miraculously allowed a girl not yet married to give birth to a baby for the sake of this world, for his created world. Isn't this the gospel Advent message? According to humanity, that is irrational. It is preposterous love that gushes and knows no bounds.

See what kind of love the Father has given to us that we should be called children of God; and so we are. The reason why the world does not know us is that it did not know him.... For this is the message that you have heard from the beginning that we should love one another.... By this we know love, that he laid down his life for us, and we ought to lay down our lives for the brothers.... Little children let us not love in word or talk, but in deed and in truth. (I John 3:1, 11, 16, 18)

A shepherd abandons ninety-nine sheep of his flock in search of the one who is lost.

This is inefficient and irresponsible.

Jesus commands we proffer the other cheek when we are struck.

This is dangerous.

He claims that to gain our life, we must first lose it.

This is senseless.

His apostle writes that our strength and stability come from our own weakness.

This is illogical.

And when his Spirit intervenes in human affairs, the result is love so tender and lavish we might find it embarrassing or scandalous if we look at it head on.

***

Dear God in heaven,

You came to earth to be with us. You came among us. Help us to laugh out loud and disbelieve this extraordinary tale if only for a moment, so we may relish the joyful ridiculousness of your love. You are never a God of hatred, but one who wants to run toward us in affection. Thank you for demonstrating this in a clearer way through your Son Jesus. Our Advent prayer is that others will see your love through us in action, and not merely in rhetoric.
Amen.

Reflections:

1. What is the most lavish demonstration of love I have witnessed? How did it affect me?
2. Why is it difficult to imagine God full of affection and love?

December 20

New

> *Oh, the joy*
> *Of young ideas painted on the mind,*
> *In the warm, glowing colors fancy spreads*
> *On objects not yet known, when all is new*
> *And all is lovely!*
>
> —Hannah More in Sacred Dramas: Chiefly Intended for Young Persons

The Bible has a very meaningful expression: The Spirit makes all things new. We are those who grow old, and we want everything done to our aged standards. The Spirit is never old; the Spirit is always young.

—Oscar Romero from a homily delivered December 17, 1978

As we wait for his coming, we grow weary. We are waiting in an old world, heavy with groaning, oppressive systems, a lack of justice, satisfaction and stability. While we wait, we see our world crumbling, we want to patch it, but we have promises for something better, beyond the comprehension of our pale imaginations. As the prophets intermittently proclaimed, we wait for the Christ to come, not just to fix what is broken, but to recreate something altogether new. As we wait, we learn trust and patience if we rest in the character of God, for we hardly know what else to expect.

So, when God came incarnate most did not recognize him. He came in the flesh, as a baby, still completely vulnerable and helpless, and it would be years before he would be able to usher in the newness. His appearance in the manger trough, however, was the promise of that newness. It is why Mary treasured the event, why Herod raged and slaughtered, and it is why the shepherds raced from the outskirts of Bethlehem rejoicing.

And I heard a loud voice from the throne saying, "Behold, the dwelling place of God is with man. He will dwell with them, and they will be his people, and God himself will be with them as their God." (Revelation 21:3)

This verse, pulled from the final book of the New Testament, is looking to his final Advent. In great anticipation we search the horizon in earnest hope for his second coming. We know he will truly and eternally dwell among his people, then. But this verse also reminds us of the initial Advent, the incarnation, connecting us to Mary and the shepherds, and the prophets long since gone, that he has come. He pitched his tent and shone the glory of the eternal I AM, while he traversed dusty trails, and shook down age-old ways of thinking and acting and being. This may be a hint as to why he always seemed to heal on the Sabbath, or touch the unclean, or speak to the "wrong" people. He was at work breaking down the old, not fixing the former institutions and systems, but recreating them. This new system would be formed on his terms, and it would make obsolete all our previous assumptions and myopic biases. His lowly birth proclaimed the start of something different.

Life, truth and reality, from now on, will be arranged in all new ways. They will be replenished; they will be a continual renewal, a life lived in constant rejuvenation, not fettered again by our fatigue, nor contingent upon our confidence.

As he struggled against the newborn cloths and pushed hungrily against his mother, his birth declared something brand new.

And he who was seated on the throne said, "Behold, I am making all things new." (Revelation 21:5)

Any newborn dismantles old ways of living, sending her parents into rejecting former priorities in exchange for new ones, but this holy infant is dismantling much more.

He knocks down the regimes of power and dominance and surprisingly builds up new means of life through peace and openness. The old systems of politics and retribution, allegiance, social relations, and ideas of scarcity are cancelled as illegitimate. In place of these,

Jesus creates new realities to be cherished. He is not concerned with overthrowing political parties or passing laws of religious liberty, but with transforming our minds for his kingdom.

The original covenant God made with his chosen people was not faulty. God never backtracked to reinvent his plan of redemption. It was maintained from the foundation of the world and was the same as the one he whispered from the Genesis garden. Jesus had always been the expected one, the solution from the mind of the Trinity.

"Do not think that I have come to abolish the Law or the Prophets; I have not come to abolish them but to fulfill them." (Matthew 5:17)

In his initial Advent Jesus did, indeed, fulfill every promise to Adam, Abraham, Moses, and beyond. Every prophet who spoke of the Assyrians or Babylonians, who spoke out for God against their own people, the Israelites, and who spoke of things to be fulfilled within their lifetime, were simultaneously speaking of the eternal One to come who would complete their words of prophecy in their highest sense.

Rather, the incarnate Word is born into the world, not to change the story, nor to destroy any of God's former designs, but to knock down the barriers and to clarify the obscurities which humanity had constructed for their own purposes. Jesus speaks of everyday items—of clothing and reusable bottles and Cabernet Sauvignon—to show us the great burden we have created for ourselves, and how greatly it has shifted our focus off the rest and the newness that he brings.

After defending his disciples from the myopia of the Pharisees regarding fasting, Jesus relates this parable:

"No one tears a piece from a new garment and puts it on an old garment. If he does, he will tear the new and the piece from the new will not match the old. And no one puts new wine into old wineskins. If he does, the new wine will burst the skins and it will be spilled, and the skins will be destroyed. But new wine must be put into fresh wineskins. And no one after drinking the old wine desires new, for he says, 'The old is good.'" (Luke 5:36-39)

Here Jesus proclaims himself to be the wine. We must not focus on the exterior things that would distract us from joyfully resting in his grace or enslave us to unsound ideas regarding his kingdom. In his Kingdom we are free to touch those with diseases (Luke 5:13); we are free to seek new ways of meeting him (Luke 5:18); and new thoughts regarding punitive systems, and the possibility of responses to forgiveness and mercy and compassion. (Luke 5:30-32). He destroys the barriers humanity has created by rejecting the concept of the "other." He affirms healing and celebration can happen on holy days, for he himself is the holy day. He is the Lord of the Sabbath, our rest and rejuvenation (Luke 6:5).

Jesus dismisses these false barriers and liberates us to act out of a sense of rebirth and plenty, free from fear and full of compassion.

There is a generative beauty and peace to the way Jesus approaches each person in Luke, chapters five and six, and indeed, throughout his ministry. He speaks of himself as rest (Matthew 11:28) and Lord of the Sabbath, (Luke 6:5), the exact day created to symbolize and provide the promise of its ultimate fulfillment at his final Advent. We rest in him, because he is our Sabbath, our wine that we will partake of together as perfect community in the Kingdom of God.

So then, there remains a Sabbath rest for the people of God, for whoever has entered God's rest has also rested from his works as God did from his. (Hebrews 4:9-10)

Because Jesus came, incarnate, clothed in complete humanity, we do not need to put our efforts in false institutions, in ill-conceived patchwork solutions, or in oppressive systems which God never designed. We rest, instead, in the exhilarating newness and restoration of his entire beloved world. His grace has accomplished the work, and now we await his glorious Advent.

***

Unchangeable Father,
Rejuvenate us. Recreate us. We rest in you.

Reflections:

1. What do I need rest from? What am I most looking forward to being restored and made new?
2. What has Jesus made new? What has he been faithful in maintaining?

December 21

No Excuses

The Christian ideal has not been tried and found wanting. It has been found difficult and left untried.

-G. K. Chesterton in What's Wrong with the World

The idea of the perfect human might differ depending on if you are coming from classical Greek thought, a Viking society, an early modern industrial nation, or twenty-first century America. However, according to the vision of God the perfect human looks like Jesus. Jesus lived with a full measure of the Holy Spirit in action and thought. To be full of God's Spirit, however, we must first empty ourselves of self, and all the narrow-minded thoughts which accompany it. As in the early Christian ballad, we read of the depths which Jesus surrendered in complete obedience to God in his life's work and in the transformation of his thoughts as a man.

Let each of you look not only to his own interests, but also to the interests of others. Have this mind among yourselves, which is yours in Christ Jesus, who though he was in the form of God, did not count equality with God a thing to be grasped, but emptied himself, by taking the form of a servant, being born in the likeness of men. And being found in human form, he humbled himself by becoming obedient to the point of death, even death on a cross. (Philippians 2:4-8)

He gave himself over to the exact mission of God, and lived fully for the "other," for the proclamation of God's sovereignty and for the gracious redemption of us all. Did he perform miracles with his own divine power, or had he surrendered that when he was fitted with his humanity and mortality? Was he so tuned in to the Holy Spirit that he was able to tap into his uncanny and mysterious power? Did Jesus grow in knowledge? Did he know he was eternal at birth? When he was lost in Jerusalem at Passover? Did he argue with his brothers? Did he sigh when Joseph asked for his help? Is sighing a sin?

This man, hailed by the prophets, loved by the masses, committed nothing against God, nor did he rebel in attitude or thought. It was for this reason we celebrate his great birth, for his birth brings all of us to life.

Since then we have a great high priest who has passed through the heavens, Jesus, the Son of God, let us hold fast our confession. For we do not have a high priest who is unable to sympathize with our

weaknesses, but one who in every respect has been tempted as we are, yet without sin.
(Hebrews 4:14-15)

We may be tempted to say here that this sinless life is not expected of us, or that it is impossible and futile to attempt, because after all, Jesus was God, and I am not. While we may sound humble, we are also tempted to rely on this as an excuse. Can I love my enemies since I am only human? Is it not unrealistic to expect me to remain patient when people threaten me? His grace, instead, compels us to be more like him.

Not only is Jesus our moral exemplar in his death as our sacrifice for sin, but he is our moral exemplar in the way he lived his life. He was not obedient in patience and truth and compassion and humor and mercy as God, but ever so much more so because he was a man. He decided on compassion because he was tired; he chose selflessness because he had ambition, too. But he knew God was to be glorified.

If we are honest, we will admit we sin, not just because we are human, but because we have not made that wilderness decision to definitively empty ourselves like Jesus did. We hold on to a bit of ourselves, and to a few reservations, unsure of what God wants to do with us.

The Hebrew writer says we can be confident in Jesus. He sympathizes with us, because he has already accomplished it. What does the perfect human look like? Look no further than the makeshift cradle in Bethlehem, to the boat with the fishermen on the Sea of Galilee, to the grief-wracked man tensed and hunched over in the garden moments before the soldiers came. Look at Jesus.

Our problem with sin has nothing to do with the fact that we are not God, but that we refuse to be emptied. What joy, what power are we, therefore, missing?

He longs to show us. As we wait for him, let us rejoice that he also shows us abundant grace and love. For the Hebrew writer also promises,

Let us then with confidence draw near to the throne of grace, that we may receive mercy and find grace to help in time of need. (Hebrews 4:16)

***

Holy Jesus, empowered by the Spirit, willing to submit utterly to the Father's will, show us how to obey. Show us how to abandon self and relinquish our human thoughts for your thoughts. We call on the Spirit's power in our lives and ask that you direct us. Thank you for being the perfect human. Show us how to reflect that to others in love and compassion.
Amen.

Reflections:

1. Where is God calling me to obey him more closely this Advent?
2. How do I think that God's grace empowers me to obey?

December 22

The Body of Christ

When ministers and priests live their ministry mostly in their heads and relate to the Gospel as a set of valuable ideas to be announced, the body quickly takes revenge by screaming loudly for affection and intimacy. Christian leaders are called to live the incarnation, that is, to live in the body, not only in their own bodies but also in the corporate body of the community, and to discover there the presence of the Holy Spirit.

-Henri Nouwen in In the Name of Jesus: Reflections on Christian Leadership

Christ didn't redeem us by a direct intellectual act, but became incarnate in human form, and he speaks to us now through the mediation of a visible Church.

-Flannery O'Connor in Mystery and Manners

The body of the Christ-child grew and developed just as any other baby boy. He learned to walk and talk. He entered adolescence, his voice deepened, and he hardened muscle from daily chores. Jesus' body entered manhood like any other, and it would be with this body that he would suffer for us, so that we might be drawn back to God, to be forever his people once more.

It may seem peculiar to be speaking of suffering and death at the Advent season. It is traditionally a time we focus on Jesus as an infant, arriving amid angelic choruses. Yet there would be no shepherds from the fields leaning in to look upon the Christ-child if God had not first planned his redemptive story through the cross.

As Jesus gathered his friends together for a final Passover meal, he celebrated with all the proper Jewish accoutrements, but perhaps with even more sobriety and bittersweet pangs than usual. He held up a loaf of bread.

When he had given thanks, he broke it and said, "This is my body, which is for you. Do this in remembrance of me." (I Corinthians 11:24)

How did his friends hear those words that night in the upper room? A broken loaf of bread? Part of a Passover meal? Something shared? How do we hear it? Certainly, we understand in a clearer way that Jesus gave his body for us as a sacrifice, as an example for us all. But do we also hear the connection the apostle Paul gives in his epistle about the body of Jesus? This bread is metaphorically the body of Christ, but now post-resurrection, post-ascension, so we also are the body of Christ. Communally, as the Church, we all comprise his holy body given for the sake of the world. Here is our charge.

For just as the body is one and has many members, and all the members of the body, though many are one body, so it is with Christ. For in one Spirit we were all baptized into one body—Jews or Greeks, slaves or free—and all were made to drink of one Spirit. For the body does not consist of one member but of many.... If one member suffers, all suffer together; if one member is honored, all rejoice together. Now you are the body of Christ and individually members of it. (I Corinthians 12:12-14, 26-27)

Jesus has returned to the Father in heaven, and as we await his final Advent, we remain as his body serving, blessing, suffering for the sake of the world and its well-being. We are not a redemptive body in the same sense that Jesus was; only his sinlessness and righteousness can be effective in that way. Nor are we the body—the hands and feet—of Christ individually. We are not meant to serve alone or in isolation. Our walk, led by his Spirit whom he left for each of us, is meant to be lived collectively, in communion, through faith where he leads.

In truth, we are not little Jesuses, but graciously, we are a part of his body. This Advent, as you sing the carols of the season in community, as you sit with your family around the tree, as you serve those who are hurting together, know it is to you Christ also speaks.

As the Immanuel rose from the Passover table, he gazed upon his friends, took the bread and said,

This is my body, which is for you. Do this in remembrance of me.

***

Holy Father,

Bless your body, the church. Create in us a love for your world and a desire to serve as your Son Jesus did. We pray that your Holy Spirit is alive and active through us. Bless us this Advent and open our eyes and hearts to see where you would lead us so that your Spirit may bless others through us.

Reflections:

1. What do I concentrate on when I participate in communion with the church? Why is it meaningful to me?
2. What are the connections between the incarnation we celebrate at Advent and the crucifixion and resurrection we celebrate at Easter?

December 23

Living Generously

Brothers, do not be afraid of man's sin, love man also in his sin, for this likeness of God's love is the height of love on earth. Love all of God's creation, both the whole of it and every grain of sand. Love every leaf, every ray of God's light. Love animals, love plants, love each thing. If you love each thing, you will perceive the mystery of God in things.

    -Fyodor Dostoevsky in The Brothers Karamazov

Life in the Spirit of Jesus is therefore a life in which Jesus' coming into the world—his incarnation, his death and resurrection—is lived out by those who have entered into the same obedient relationship to the Father which marked Jesus' own life. Having become sons and daughters as Jesus was Son, our lives become a continuation of Jesus' mission.

    -Henri Nouwen in Making All Things New

Living generously as the body of Christ, we emulate Jesus' own attitude and actions. When he shows compassion for the marginalized, so do we. When he devotes his time to serving others, so do we. When he spends time concentrated in prayer, or listening to someone who has interrupted his day, so do we. Of course, I say we do this as the Church as a hopeful prayer. As the body of Christ, we ought to be acting in such ways. Normatively, this is who the Church is. Would our friends and neighbors experience this as a startling anomaly? Or would they define a follower of Jesus in precisely these ways? As Henri Nouwen explained "our lives become a continuation of Jesus' mission."

In his great love for us, God was generous in sending his Son to move among us. During his life Jesus was characterized by his generosity. He was one of us, but he lived full of lavish graciousness, yet as a servant. Jesus lived generously, forfeiting many of his own interests. He lived for the sake of others, but primarily for God's mission. We are also to live generously in every aspect of our life. The apostle Paul does not leave out any corner of our life when he challenges the Roman Christians.

Love one another with brotherly affection. Outdo one another in showing honor. Do not be slothful in zeal, be fervent in spirit, serve the Lord. Rejoice in hope, be patient in tribulation, be constant in prayer. Contribute to the needs of the saints and seek to show hospitality.

Bless those who persecute you; bless and do not curse them. Rejoice with those who rejoice, weep with those who weep. Live in harmony with one another. Do not be haughty, but associate with the lowly. Never be wise in your own sight. Repay no one evil for evil, but give thought to do what is honorable in the sight of all. If possible, so far as it depends on you, live peaceably with all…. Do not be overcome by evil, but overcome evil with good. (Romans 12:10-18, 21)

During Advent, donate generously to charities. Invite someone to dinner. Listen to the concerns of others. Give people the benefit of the doubt. We are called to be generous with our money, but we also follow Christ by opening our hearts to giving time, gratitude, hospitality, peaceableness, honor, prayer and thoughts of goodwill to others. Do we assume others have good intentions, or do we participate in reactive accusations? Do we know how to listen with kindness and warm-heartedness when others disagree with us? That is generosity. Can we accept differences without fear? That is generosity. Can we give an hour of our time to a menial task we think unimportant? That is generosity. Can we speak words of genuine gratefulness, or do we assume others are just doing their job? The body of Christ is for service and we live in unspeakably generous ways.

Do we open our homes to neighbors? Are we able to make space for the lonely? Do we view our home, cars, freedom, our lifestyle as blessings we are grateful for, or as our personal possessions we have earned? Jesus lived for the sake of others and so must we as his Church. Living generously means living within God's plenty. We are children of a Father who knows no scarcity of love or grace, no scarcity of mercy or compassion. Even our thoughts presume an attitude of inclusivity. We gather others around us because we are confident there is enough. We share with those in need, with those who are hurting, with those who mourn, who need support, who despise us, who treat us with contempt, who try to grab from us what they can. Jesus is loving, and he shows us the Father's arms are always open.

He saw the rich young ruler.

> Jesus, looking at him, loved him. (Mark 10:21)

He was not afraid to touch people, nor was he repulsed by the unwanted.

> When Jesus saw her, he called her over and said to her, "Woman, you are freed from your disability." And he laid his hands on her, and immediately she was made straight. (Luke 13:12-13)

> And a leper came to him.... Moved with pity, he stretched out his hand and touched him. (Mark 1:40-41)

He identified with the pain of others and felt the searing loss of death.

> Jesus wept.

So the Jews said, "See how he loved him!" (John 11:35-36)

Even in the face of his own death he spoke from plenty. He forgave.

And Jesus said, "Father, forgive them, for they know not what they do." (Luke 23:34)

His incarnate body was for taking on service and suffering and death. "By his wounds we are healed" (Isaiah 53:5). Such generosity! It is generosity that compels us to do the same.
***

Jesus,
Although we celebrate your birth and your incarnation at this time of year, we also know your mission includes serving others. We pray your Spirit enlivens us with your peaceableness, your fierce generosity and tender love for all we encounter. Take away our need to hold on to our reputations, our money and possessions, or our need to be right. Make us a generous people.
In your holy name,
Amen.

Reflections:

1. Who is the most generous person I know? How have they arranged their life to be able to demonstrate this generosity?
2. In what ways am I generous? Where do I need to grow in generosity?

December 24

Holy Spirit

But there was a Being, spirit, infinite, I AM. In that being there was One and there were many. There was Love. There was Joy. There was true Laughter. There was a Word, a Voice. There was Artist, but there was not yet art.

And that Voice said Light, and extended Himself a finite canvas to paint the only thing that could be worth painting, to paint the I AM.

The art has a beginning—it began when time did—but it will have no end. Only endings. Even now it still grows and expands, twists and intertwines, rises and sets, spins and doubles back.

The Voice will never be silent.

-N. D. Wilson in Notes from the Tilt-a-Whirl: Wide-Eyed Wonder in God's Spoken World

On this eve before Christ's Advent, we focus our thoughts on the One who is traditionally named as the third person in the Trinity, the Holy Spirit. It is right that we should so train our minds, for when something new is on the cusp there is always the Spirit. In fact, we will see that God's Holy Spirit plays an integral role in creating, gifting, renewing and proclaiming God's narrative. From before time was created, the Spirit of God hovered over the waters (Genesis 1:2). In the void and darkness, we imagine divinity like a bird skimming the surface, wings splayed out, trembling with an exuberant expectancy. What will become? God does not disappoint us in the first chapters of Scripture, nor does he disappoint us in Luke's opening account of the Gospel. The Spirit is everywhere in the events leading to incarnation and nativity.

Luke 1:15: Here the angel reveals to Zechariah that his son John, who will impossibly be conceived in old age, will be filled with the Holy Spirit. In the same chapter (Luke 1:41), Zechariah's wife Elizabeth is filled with the Holy Spirit on meeting the expecting Mary. John would play a pivotal role in preparing the world for an incarnated God.

Luke 1:35: Gabriel's appearance to Mary is no less startling than the message of incarnation through her own body. The Holy Spirit will overshadow Mary so she will carry God with her. This divine shadow-casting reminds us of the imagery of the Spirit hovering over the water. The Spirit hovered at the creation of all the world. Later, when the Lord created his holy nation of people at Mount Sinai, he established his presence by hovering or settling on the tent of meeting. His glory filled it.

Then the cloud covered the tent of meeting, and the glory of the Lord filled the tabernacle. And Moses was not able to enter the tent of meeting because the cloud settled on it, and the glory of the Lord filled the tabernacle. (Exodus 40:34-35)

He hovered over Mary, overshadowing her, as the Trinity created something new through the incarnation. It was the tent pitched among us. Jesus was now one of us. Because of the work of the Holy Spirit, his glory walked the earth full of grace and truth.

Luke 1:67: At John's birth, Zechariah was filled with the Holy Spirit and prophesied, explaining the redemptive plan of God.

Luke 2:25-27: Simeon is a beautiful example of God gifting people for the sake of his own mission. This man, now elderly, seems to be surrounded at every turn by the Spirit's gifts of power. As Simeon waits, the Holy Spirit is upon him, revealing the truth of the incarnation to him, promising him his own role in the story, and being present with him, guiding him into the temple at just the right time. There was God-incarnate eight days old!

Luke 3:21-22: Jesus' baptism by John marked the beginning of his ministry. When the Holy Spirit, not only hovered but descended on Jesus, he hailed him as the One who was to come. From this time on, Jesus is described as being full of the Holy Spirit (Luke 4:1) and acting out of the power of the Holy Spirit (Luke 4:14).

Now, as we live in the overlap, between grace and glory, how do we trust in the Spirit's movement to fall upon us, guide us, call us, recreate us and fill us with his power? After all, we are his people, created and formed collectively as a Church, for good works for the sake of all. Jesus' entire life and ministry was characterized by the power of the Holy Spirit. His people reflect the same power. At Advent we sing praise for the grace of his first appearing, the incarnation of Immanuel. At Advent we also turn our eyes ahead and praise him proleptically in the glory of his endmost Advent. He is coming, but as we wait, we trust in the empowering promise he left for us, his Holy Spirit.

Like Jesus, we are also filled with this power, equipped for generative and loving actions for his church and the whole world. When a life is transformed, when fear is cast aside, and new, peaceable attitudes emerge, the Holy Spirit is always present. He creates, proclaims, empowers. The incarnation would have been impossible without him. We await expectantly to see what he will create for us and through us this Advent season.

But when the goodness and loving kindness of God our Savior appeared, he saved us, not because of works done by us in righteousness, but according to his own mercy, by the washing of regeneration and renewal of the Holy Spirit, whom he poured out on us richly

through Jesus Christ our Savior, so that being justified by his grace we might become heirs according to the hope of eternal life. (Titus 3:4-7)
***

Holy Spirit,
Prepare us for your creative presence. Help us to see the world as you do. Work in us and through us as your people.
O Lord hear our prayer.

Reflections:

1. Have I noticed the Holy Spirit working in other believers' lives? Have I been attentive to the Holy Spirit speaking or working through me?
2. What other passages of Scripture show us the Holy Spirit hovering or creating something new?

December 25

Christmas Day

Moonless darkness stands between,
Past, the Past, no more be seen.
But the Bethlehem star may lead me
To the sight of Him who freed me
From the self that I have been.
Make me pure, Lord: Thou art holy;
Make me meek, Lord: Thou wert lowly;
Now beginning, and always,
Now begin, on Christmas day.

          -Gerard Manley Hopkins in "Christmas Prayer"

Whether you are reading this early in the morning with your coffee before the kids come screaming downstairs ready to tear away wrapping and bows, or quietly, alone, at the end of the day, I pray you have the peace and hope the Lord fully intends for you. He came that you might know him, that he might be with you.

For the grace of God has appeared bringing salvation for all people, training us to renounce ungodliness and worldly passions, and to live self-controlled, upright and godly lives in the present age, waiting for our blessed hope, the appearing of the glory of our great God and Savior Jesus Christ, who gave himself for us to redeem us from all lawlessness and to purify for himself a people for his own possession who are zealous for good works. (Titus 2:11-14)

Today we celebrate the grace that appeared over two thousand years ago, heralded by angels, bringing the hope of salvation for the world. Jesus has come just as he promised. His coming was the renewal of all things. It was gentleness and grace. One day there will be a different appearing. He will come again, but this time in the glory of God. His subsequent coming will also usher in something new. There will be a gathering, a redemption and a victory that will make all the waiting and preparation worthwhile.

Now, as we continue to wait, we are in training. We look to Jesus for ways of being holy. We know rightness and gentleness, kindness and graciousness are not found in abundance in the world. Jesus, however, both the holy one and lowly one, demonstrates how we practice these things. He trusts in his Father, he submits to his parents, he relies on the power of the Holy Spirit and he is patient as he grows in wisdom. We look at Jesus because we want to reflect his beautiful truth. Transformation takes time, but we strive to give credibility and beauty to the gospel.

On Christmas Day, we have the blessed hope. Jesus' birth provides us with the hope of God exacting justice on the garden serpent, the hope of redeeming us back into communion with him. Again, we wait and prepare for a final Advent. We have the blessed hope of Christ's final coming. He will not only come to live in our midst but gather us all up as his people. This time we will live with God, and he will be among us.

We live between the two appearances. We live in between grace and glory. The grace of God brought tender salvation. The glory of God will bring joyous reunification.

Glory to God in the highest.

Immanuel. God will be with us.

***

Dear Jesus, Son of God,
You came full of grace and truth, and you will return in glory, in unexpected ways at an unexpected time. Help us to train well and to reflect even a mere glimmer of your glory. We long to shine brightly with your gentleness and inclusivity, with your justice and kindliness and humanity.
Come, Lord Jesus.

Reflections:

1. As we wait, what do I think the world needs from me the most? How is the Holy Spirit equipping me to provide it?
2. Transformation takes time. What spiritual disciplines will benefit me the most this season? Bible study? Prayer? Meditation? Journaling? Fasting?

December 26

Final Advent

The world is dark, and light is precious.
Come closer, dear reader.
You must trust me.
I am telling you a story.
   -Kate DiCamillo in The Tale of Despereaux

Hope is being able to see that there is light despite all of the darkness.
   -Desmond Tutu from "The Priest," a March 4, 2010 interview in The New York Times Magazine

This morning we might awake to a sense of disappointment or disillusionment. The holiday has past and we don't always feel we have done enough. Living between the appearances of grace and glory can be discouraging. One has already been fulfilled, yet the other seems so far off. He has come. We rejoiced for a time, but again we hurt, again we feel the oppression of injustice, the stifling attitude of entitlement and scarcity. We mourn our own selfishness, questioning whether or not he came in vain. What do we do on the days of the overlap, when Jesus' final coming is yet to be realized? How do we wait and prepare? As the Hebrew writer encourages us, we keep our eyes on the promised One, the One the prophets foretold, the One the angels heralded (Hebrews 12:1-2). The One who is coming is faithful. We trust in his promise. He is better than the angels, better than the prophet-like-me, better than the law, better than Moses, better than the sacrificial system. He is better than hard work and our "barely enoughs."

Therefore do not throw away your confidence, which has a great reward. For you have need of endurance, so that when you have done the will of God you may receive what is promised. For,

"Yet a little while,
and the coming one will come and
> will not delay;
but my righteous one shall live by
> faith,
and if he shrinks back,
my soul has no pleasure in him." (Hebrews 10:35-38)

We are tired from waiting. We get lost in the daily distractions. We become entangled in the same insipid sins. How do we know he will come? We see violence and are short on peace. We hear accusations and aggressions, and still long for simple affability. We remember Jesus' kindness. We remember Mary's trust. We remember shepherds in a field, cousins' shared joy. We remember a journey. We remember hundreds of years of waiting. And he came. Will he come again making all things new as he promised?

Can we rest in exuberant hopefulness for this final Advent? Do we celebrate his once-upon-a-time birth, but doubt his inevitable return?

But we are not of those who shrink back and are destroyed, but of those who have faith and preserve their souls. (Hebrews 10:39)

May we be open to receiving the divine in our life today. May we be open to recognizing the blessings and the light, just as the wise men recognized the bright, auspicious star. May we make room for him as we make room for the others before us who need a place to stay, a warm meal, an accepting word, a sympathetic ear. Are we ready to welcome him back as we welcome others into our lives? We awaited this first Advent. As we await the final Advent, may we grow into a reflection of Immanuel's abiding love.

May the Lord make you increase and abound in love for one another and for all, as we do for you, so that he may establish your hearts blameless in holiness before our God and Father, at the coming of our Lord Jesus with all his saints. (I Thessalonians 3:12-13)

***

Returning Lord,

Come in your grace and glory. Make us your forever people again. Increase our gentleness in a hateful world. Increase our faith in your coming. We proclaim your promise that you will pitch your tent and live with us in your glory. God, you will be among us.

Amen.

Reflections:

1. After the holiday is past, what am I most looking forward to? What simple beauty am I anticipating in my ordinary, daily life?
2. What has been a particularly meaningful part of this Advent for me? What will I choose to remember from this season?

BIOGRAPHICAL NOTES

Maya Angelou (1928—2014) - American poet and civil rights activist. She is also known for her memoirs and autobiographies, the first of which is *I Know Why the Caged Bird Sings* (1969).

Athanasius of Alexandria (296—373 AD) - Christian theologian and early Church Father. He defended the biblical concept of Trinity and the divinity of Jesus.

Augustine of Hippo (354—430 AD) - Christian theologian and philosopher. Bishop of Hippo Regius in modern day Algeria. He is best known for his *Confessions* and *The City of God*.

Karl Barth (1886—1968) - Swiss theologian. He is known for his commentary *The Epistle to the Romans*, and was involved with the Confessing Church, which opposed Nazi government and worked to unify all Protestant denominations. He significantly influenced Dietrich Bonhoeffer, Reinhold Niebuhr and many others.

Wendell Berry (born 1934) - poet, novelist, essayist, agriculturalist, environmental activist. He lives and farms in rural Kentucky. His novels center around the fictionalized town of Port William, and describe the community of people there, who refer to themselves as the "membership."

Dietrich Bonhoeffer (1906—1945) - German pastor, theologian and founding member of the Confessing Church. He is best known for his meditative and theological works, particularly *Life Together* and *The Cost of Discipleship*. He was executed by the Nazis in April 1945 for involvement in a plot to assassinate Adolf Hitler.

Walter Brueggeman (born 1933) - Old Testament scholar and theologian. His work concentrates on reimagining the modern day Church free of nationalism, militarism and consumerism. His works include *The Prophetic Imagination* (1978), *Spirituality of the Psalms* (2001) and *Sabbath as Resistance: Saying No to the Culture of NOW* (2014).

Frederick Buechner (born 1926) - poet, novelist, preacher, theologian. His best-known work of fiction is *Godric* (1981). His works *Telling the Truth* (1977), *The Sacred Journey* (1982), and most recently *Secrets in the Dark: A Life in Sermons* (2006) include memoirs, sermons and essays. He is most noted for his imaginative story-telling style even when discussing theology and biblical events.

G. K. Chesterton (1874—1936) - English poet, essayist, biographer, philosopher, Christian apologist, literary critic. He is known for his humorous detective stories involving the priest Father Brown. His

Christian apologetic work includes *Orthodoxy* (1908) and *The Everlasting Man* (1925).

Kate DiCamillo (born 1964) - American writer of children's fiction. Winner of two Newberry Medals. Known for providing children with emotionally rich stories full of hopeful endings. Works include *Because of Winn Dixie*, *The Tale of Despereaux* and *The Miraculous Journey of Edward Tulane*.

Shusaku Endo (1923—1996) - Japanese author. He converted to Roman Catholicism as a boy, but maintained an interest in other religions, namely Buddhism. His distinctive religious perspective made him controversial both in Japan and internationally. His most famous novel is *Silence* (1966), which deals with the persecution of Portuguese missionaries in Edo-era Japan. He narrowly missed winning the Nobel Prize in 1994 to Kenzaburo Oe.

Makoto Fujimura (born 1960) - Japanese American abstract or non-representational artist. He is known for his colorful and modern use of nihonga, an ancient Japanese technique which uses pigments from minerals and semi-precious stones. He is the founder of Fujimura Institute, and was commissioned in 2009 by Crossway Publishing to illuminate the four Gospels in commemoration of the 400th anniversary of the King James Bible. His Christian faith is evident in all his work. In his book *Culture Care* (2017) he describes the need for artists to be "border-stalkers" in order to help create the positive, flourishing culture the world needs.

O. Henry (1862—1910) - American short story writer. He led a colorful, if not morally questionable, life. His stories range from urban and industrial settings to lonely Western ranch lands far from civilization. They are invariably characterized by their surprise endings.

Gerard Manley Hopkins (1844—1889) - English poet and Jesuit priest. His poetry greatly influenced T. S. Eliot, as well as others. He is particularly known for his rich imagery and sprung rhythm, the imitation of natural speech. Faith in God and evidence of him in nature are two of his common poetic themes.

John Henry Hopkins, Jr. (1820—1891) - American Episcopal bishop. He is best known for the hymn "We Three Kings," (1857) which he wrote for his nieces and nephews to perform in their Christmas pageant.

Martin Luther King, Jr. (1929—1968) - American Baptist preacher and pacifist leader in the Civil Rights Movement. He is known for his "I Have a Dream" speech delivered in 1963 in Washington D.C. during the Civil Rights March, among other speeches, writings, and activity. He was assassinated in Memphis, Tennessee, on April 4, 1968.

Min Jin Lee (born 1968) - Korean American writer. Her novels often deal with the themes of belonging and identity, and to a certain extent, faith. They include *Free Food for Millionaires* (2007) and *Pachinko* (2017).

Madeleine L'Engle (1918—2007) - beloved children's author and essayist. Her works frequently showcase her respect for children, her interest in science and her Christian faith. She is undoubtedly best known for *A Wrinkle in Time*, the first novel in a five-part series.

C. S. Lewis (1898—1963) - professor of Medieval Studies and English literature at Oxford University and, later, Cambridge University. He is arguably best known as a beloved lay theologian and children's author. He was good friends with J. R. R. Tolkien and co-founder of the Inklings, a literary support group. His best-known works may be *The Screwtape Letters* (1942), *Mere Christianity* (1952), and his *The Chronicles of Narnia* series (1950-1956).

Thomas Merton (1915—1968) - American Trappist monk, theologian, social activist, mystic and scholar of comparative religions. He had a particular interest in Buddhism. Although born in France, he spent most of his adult life in Kentucky at the Abbey of Gethsemani near Bardstown, Kentucky. He is known for his spiritual memoir *The Seven Storey Mountain* (1948).

Joseph Mohr (1792—1848) - Austrian Roman Catholic priest who penned the lyrics to the beloved Christmas poem "Silent Night" (1816). Two years later his friend, Franz Gruber wrote the accompanying music so it could be used at a Christmas Eve midnight Mass.

Hannah More (1745—1833) - English philanthropist, religious writer, poet, playwright, abolitionist. She was a member of the literary Bluestocking group and worked tirelessly and closely with William Wilberforce to eradicate slavery in England.

Henri Nouwen (1932—1996) - Dutch Catholic priest, theologian and pastoral minister. He lived in Ontario until his death as a member of a communal group called L'Arche, which is devoted to the acceptance and spiritual care of people with developmental disabilities.

Flannery O'Connor (1925—1964) - American Catholic writer of short stories, novels and essays. Her Southern Gothic stories are filled with biblical and religious imagery, shocking scenes of cruelty and revelation, but all for the purpose of revealing the need for Christ's stunning grace in each of our lives. Her stories include "A Good Man is Hard to Find," "Revelation" and "Good Country People." She died prematurely after suffering for years from lupus.

Katherine Paterson (born 1932) - American children's author and essayist. Her award-winning books include *Bridge to Terabithia* (1977), *The Great Gilly Hopkins* (1978), and *Jacob Have I Loved* (1980).

Alan Paton (1903—1988) - South African author and anti-apartheid activist. His novel *Cry, the Beloved Country* (1948) did much to humanize and draw attention to the injustice of racial prejudices and attempted to act as a warning to the world.

Marilynne Robinson (born 1943) - American novelist and essayist. She was awarded the Pulitzer Prize for Fiction in 2005, primarily for her best-known work *Gilead*. Her novels *Home* (2008) and *Lila* (2014), while not exactly part of a series, loosely relate with overlapping characters. Her slow-moving, introspective writing is beautiful and covers themes like family, redemption, forgiveness, faith and religion.

Oscar Romero (1917—1980) - Archbishop of San Salvador, El Salvador, and spokesperson for social justice. He was assassinated while celebrating Mass in the chapel of the Hospital of Divine Providence for his insistence on pacifism and for voicing protests against death squad slaughters during the civil war in El Salvador.

S. D. Smith (born 1977) - Author of the middle grade novel series *The Green Ember,* which chronicles the valiant adventures of the rabbits of Natalia as they fight against wolves and birds of prey to restore peace and reestablish the Mended Wood. Smith is also a contributor to the Story Warren, a publishing company and website created to "foster imagination in children."

Desmond Tutu (born 1931) - South African Anglican cleric and anti-apartheid activist. Was Archbishop of Capetown from 1986 - 1996.

Simone Weil (1909—1943) - Catholic French philosopher, writer, mystic and political activist. Much of her short life was filled with social activism out of sympathy with the working class. Her writings deal with the themes of theodicy, grace and the intrinsic nature of evil in the world. *Gravity and Grace* is one of her most widely read.

Isabel Wilkerson (born 1961) – Pulitzer Prize winning American journalist and writer. She authored *The Warmth of Other Suns: The Epic Story of America's Great Migration* (2010).

N. D. Wilson (born 1978) - American author of children's and young adult fiction. His books are influenced by mythologies, contain unusual heroes with a sense of wonder in the everyday, as well as elements of horror and suspense. He has written several series, the best known being *100 Cupboards*. In his spiritual non-fiction book *Notes from the Tilt-a-Whirl* (2009) he discusses his views on faith and God in a lyrical style.

John Wesley Work, Jr. (1871—1925) - African American collector of folk songs and spirituals. He published many slave songs, hymns and spirituals in his collections, including "Go Tell It on the Mountain," which he may have partially written.

www.ingramcontent.com/pod-product-compliance
Lightning Source LLC
Chambersburg PA
CBHW071509040426
42444CB00008B/1557